Interfaith Grit

Interfaith Grit

How Uncertainty Will Save Us

STEPHANIE VARNON-HUGHES

WIPF & STOCK · Eugene, Oregon

INTERFAITH GRIT
How Uncertainty Will Save Us

Copyright © 2018 Stephanie Varnon-Hughes. All rights reserved. Except for brief quotations in critical publications or reviews, no part of this book may be reproduced in any manner without prior written permission from the publisher. Write: Permissions, Wipf and Stock Publishers, 199 W. 8th Ave., Suite 3, Eugene, OR 97401.

Wipf & Stock
An Imprint of Wipf and Stock Publishers
199 W. 8th Ave., Suite 3
Eugene, OR 97401

www.wipfandstock.com

PAPERBACK ISBN: 978-1-5326-0645-8
HARDCOVER ISBN: 978-1-5326-0647-2
EBOOK ISBN: 978-1-5326-0646-5

Manufactured in the U.S.A. MARCH 7, 2018

To Caleb Bagheera Varnon-Hughes, the bravest boy we know.
And to my husband, for being willing to travel through all of
the shaky places, together.

"The minute we begin to think we have all the answers,
we forget the questions."

—Madeleine L'Engle

Contents

Introduction | *ix*

Fear, Curiosity, Change, and Growth: The Challenges of Being Human | 1

The Problem: Our World Just Won't Stay Still | 13

Time for Pause: The Breath that Will Sustain Us | 46

Practice, Posture, and Possibility: How to Practice a Posture of Openness | 78

Imagination and Seeing with New Eyes: The Power of Storytelling | 84

In Conclusion: Will Uncertainty Save Us? | 113

Bibliography | *115*

Introduction

I started doing interfaith work because of my students. In public school in St. Louis, Missouri, my eighth graders were curious, noisy, involved, and came from all over the world.

When I taught August Wilson's *The Piano Lesson*, and we got to the part about Sutter's ghost, a Muslim student from Somali raised her hand and asked, "Miss? What happens if a woman who is pregnant dies?" Suddenly, every student in the room had an opinion, an idea, a question. Hands shot up and urgent conversations began. As a first year teacher, I wasn't ready to talk about death, but I thought—if I'm interested in teaching "the whole student," shouldn't I meet them where they are? Shouldn't I let them express their ideas about their own interior space, and ethical and religious beliefs, and learn from one another?

I became convinced that my students deserved to know why DeAnthony was fasting for Ramadan, why Jeremiah couldn't watch movies or plays that had magic in them, why some of their classmates wore headscarves and others didn't celebrate birthdays, and that learning how to talk about one's own interior space and ask questions of others respectfully and humanely were the very skills eighth grade humans needed to learn and practice.

Later, at Union Theological Seminary, I had the opportunity to imagine a free, online, peer-reviewed, academic journal for interfaith studies. I met a then-rabbinical student, Joshua Stanton,

Introduction

and together we founded *The Journal of Inter-Religious Studies*. Many of my mentors, teachers, and collaborators were involved in that project, and have gone on to help me along this path of scholarship and teaching. When I began to think about further academic work, I had the opportunity to get a PhD in inter-religious education: a new field for a new time. Teaching, learning, storytelling, listening, and relationship are cornerstones of my education, and of my practice.

This book is meant for every family member, colleague, and airplane seatmate who has asked me a variation of the following question: "Why is the world like this? And what can I do?"

Being human is a messy endeavor. We are made to be in relationship—built for community, craving to be known and seen and heard, better together. And yet, some flaw in us allows us to dwell on difference and allow diversity to become divisiveness. We fear the unknown. We resist the new. We turn strident and hateful when made to change. Why is this?

I believe that leaning into the unknown is a transformative skill. We can practice becoming okay with difference. We can become *virtuosic* at embracing the unknown. When we learn that diversity will indeed transform us in body, soul, and nation, we can systematically name, teach, and celebrate the practices that help us persevere in shaky places.

Parts of this book are based on research I did as a doctoral student, seeking to learn from scholars and practitioners in higher education about what exemplifies interfaith learning on their campuses. One section of this book helps us understand the idea of "resilience" and why it's an essential ingredient in interfaith learning. Another section explores reflective practice as a too-infrequently used skill that has powerful potential to help us flourish. Finally, there are frequent examples of tools and techniques you can use immediately in your everyday life—in your workplace, congregation, community, or family—to help become okay with uncertainty, and allow a posture of openness to deepen your engagement with others, with your own ethical or spiritual tradition, and with humanity.

Fear, Curiosity, Change, and Growth
The Challenges of Being Human

You're in a new parents group at your child's middle school. You've really hit it off with some of the parents; it feels great to have made good "parent friends" and for your child to have another source of community connected to school.

You invite one of the women to Starbucks with you after a meeting to plan for the fall bazaar, and she comes, but when she shows up, doesn't order anything. "Even water?" you ask. "Even water," she says, smiling, "It's Ramadan."

Multiple emotions and thoughts flood your brain and body at the same time:

- Cool! I have a Muslim friend! I'm progressive and inclusive.
- Oh, crap: how did I just invite a fasting person out for coffee and not know?
- Why did she come if she can't eat or drink anything?
- Is she going to think I'm terrible if *I* eat or drink something?
- How long is Ramadan? Can I ask? I'm an educated person, I should probably know . . .
- Why doesn't she wear a veil? Can I ask her that? Probably not.

- I don't want to make her uncomfortable, I'll just act like she's just like me.
- I wonder if she has any ultra-conservative family members or friends. (I can't believe I just thought that!)
- I wonder if she's ever been discriminated against.
- Wait, what does she think about all of my jokes about wine and "Mommy's Sippee Cup"?—she must think I'm really sinful or something.
- The next time I see something anti-Muslim on Facebook, I can't wait to tell my family that they are Islamophobic and I know plenty of perfectly wonderful Muslim people.
- Does she hate America?
- Curiosity
- Fear
- Interest
- Pride
- Stress that you'll make a mistake
- Embarrassment

And you think all of these thoughts and feel all of these emotions *within seconds.*

To most adults, stress—even good stress—doesn't feel good. We get butterflies in our stomachs, our hearts race, our palms or bodies get sweaty, we might feel tongue-tied, our minds race. This is dissonance, this is disequilibrium: a shaky feeling of uncertainty.

In contrast, young children experience disequilibrium all day long. They learn depth perception and object permanence, they fall and learn to navigate steps and different kinds of flooring, they are faced with differences in food and language throughout the day. They're used to not knowing. Feeling uncertain as they encounter new things is a semi-permanent state.

We adults like to believe we have it all figured out. We are masters of our little worlds, and know what we like and how to successfully navigate life with minimum confusion, stress, uncertainty, or failure. At least, this is so often our goal—and the world of self-help, religious and ethical leadership, renewal retreats, and professional development often seek to impart new information and new practices with minimum risk or discomfort. And in our rapidly interconnecting world, where we bump up against new ideas and people dozens of times per hour, we can either choose to be paralyzed by fear of the new, or understand that exposure to difference can lead to learning that will transform us: body, soul, and nation. This book is intended for activists, practitioners, and leaders in religious and inter-religious work. They may have some academic background (like having an MDiv), but this book is intended to be both framework and toolkit. Definitions for "interfaith," "alterity," "disequilibrium," and "resilience" will be given, and author's original research on resilience as a key ingredient for interfaith learning will be shared. That said, this book is intended to be useful and to make a difference in general readers' lives.

Seen on social media, February 2017:

> "I've never unfriended a person for disagreeing with me, and I've even argued for why I should keep someone on my friend's list with a vastly different worldview. However, when I've tried to be reasonable, show compassion, offer different ways of understanding, and he chooses to post something condescending and hateful about me specifically, I get to let him go and to let him live on in his echo chamber of ignorance. #selfcare #somepeopledontwantaconversation #letthemgo #breathe"

Underneath an Islamophobic video, a friend had written, tagging her publicly:

"Becky Smith[1] is killing me with her Islamophobia! I'm tryin to find all the shit I can and jam it up her Muslim lovin ass!"

Another mutual friend approved, commenting:

"Keep it up! Lol!"

These messages were not from strangers. These messages were written by people she'd known for years. In recent years, after

---

1. Not her real name.

sharing news of her marriage to a Muslim man, she had remained "friends" with them. As an interfaith leader, and person who believes in compassion and the transformative power of education, she had tried to remain committed to being in relationship with them for two reasons. First, she believed it did her good to understand what others believed, especially those with different perspectives from her. Second, she believed that her friendship with them could help them learn about difference. As she pointed out, their friendship with her, and ability to see the posts and information she shares about Islam in America, might be the only accurate information they get about Islam, or immigrants.

Is all difference good? Are there limits to engagement?

Mail received, on paper headed with the Trump presidential campaign logo, (hand delivered by a neighbor in a suburban town in the American southwest), shared on social media, November 2016:

> "Dear Terrorist-Bitch,
>
> We are writing to you as the newly organized Neighborhood Town Watch. We understand that you currently wear a scarf on your head, and we would like to put you on notice that this will no longer be tolerated in our neighborhood. Now that America is great again, we would like to offer you two opportunities to avoid any consequences of your poor previous decisions. First, you can take your radical attire of [sic] and live like all Americans. Or, your second option, you can go back to the God Forsaken land you came from. America is Great Again, Neighborhood Town Watch."

Note, the recipient of the letter was born in America. (Does that make a difference?)

People who are interested in doing interfaith work come to this arena for a variety of reasons. Some of us believe interfaith engagement is a natural outgrowth of our own spiritual commitments. For example, many religious systems include an imperative like, "Love your neighbor" or the Golden Rule.

Here are some examples of the Golden Rule from a variety of philosophical and religious systems:

Bahá'í Faith: "Ascribe not to any soul that which thou wouldst not have ascribed to thee, and say not that which thou doest not."

Brahmanism: "This is the sum of Dharma [duty]: Do naught unto others which would cause you pain if done to you."

Buddhism: "Hurt not others in ways that you yourself would find hurtful."

Christianity: "And as ye would that others should do to you, do ye also to them likewise."

Confucianism: "Do not do to others what you do not want them to do to you."

Ancient Egyptian: "Do for one who may do for you, that you may cause him or her thus to do."

Hinduism: "This is the sum of duty: do not do to others what would cause pain if done to you."

Islam: "None of you [truly] believes until he or she wishes for your brothers or sisters what you wish for yourselves."

Jainism: "Humans should wander about treating all creatures as they themselves would be treated."

Judaism: "What is hateful to you, do not to your fellow human. This is the law: all the rest is commentary."

Taoism: "Regard your neighbor's gain as your gain, and your neighbor's loss as your own loss."

Zoroastrianism: "Whatever is disagreeable to yourself do not do unto others."

Why are we emboldened online to be the worst versions of ourselves? It's likely that the men and women who wrote the posts quoted above, and who wrote and shared the "neighborhood watch" letter, consider themselves Christian to some degree. Maybe they go to church, at least for Christmas, Easter, or for weddings and funerals. Part of what many Trump supporters believe makes America "great" is a return to a nostalgic yet nonexistent status as a "Christian" country. What do we, as a general public, believe that it means to be "great" or "Christian"? Is it possible that these two ideas might be at odds?

The Golden Rule seems, in every example, to be an exhortation to do two things. First, we must know or reflect on what we would want. Do we wish to be welcomed? To be safe? To have a home and a way to provide for our families? To have the rights to study, speak, and participate in community?

And yet, many of us don't know what it is we want. Magazines, advertisements, and lifestyle blogs exist to help us determine our needs, our personal brand, the diet and exercise regimen that is right for us, and how we should marry and parent. Are we minimalist brides? Helicopter parents? Frugal, organic families? Soccer moms or tailgate dads? *Who are we*? Two of the most important therapeutic questions we can ask ourselves are: "How am I feeling?" and "What do I need?"

How am I feeling? Am I overwhelmed? Hungry? Angry? Nervous? Entitled? Jealous? Confused? Concerned?

When I see a high school friend sharing pro-Islam ideas on Facebook, how am I feeling? Am I afraid? Impressed? Jealous? Angry? Uncomfortable? Confused?

What do I need? To be the right one? To delete and retreat? To pray or meditate? To reassure myself that there are good people in the world? To lash out? To try and convince? To unfriend? To mobilize politically? To shame her? To be reassured that I am safe?

When I see that one of my neighbors has a good university job, a newish car, frequent NBA tickets to see the local hometown team, a pretty wife, and a healthy child—and he wears some kind of head covering and has a beard, how am I feeling? Confused? Jealous? Worried? Surprised? Afraid? Nostalgic for another kind of neighborhood? Competitive?

What do I need? A better job? A happier marriage? Reassurance that my community isn't changing? Reassurance that if my community changes, I'll still play an important part? Health care and good schools for my own children? A sense of certainty? To be reassured that the things that are important won't change?

Fear, Curiosity, Change, and Growth

When I see that my pastor is being attacked on Facebook by anti-Islam commenters, how am I feeling? Angry? Surprised? Embarrassed? Self-righteous? Certain? Smug? Afraid?

What do I need? To prove publicly that I am an ally? To console her? To teach her friends that they are wrong? To feel safe online? To know that diversity (even beliefs I don't agree with) is still a good thing?

When I see that my coworker has been threatened by a so-called neighborhood watch group, how am I feeling? Outraged? Surprised? Confused? Disbelieving? Disappointed?

What do I need? To let him know not all white people or Christians believe like that? To mobilize politically? To apologize? To buy a gun? To be reassured that our community really is affirming?

For many of us, when we're consuming digital media, we're moving, acting, and reacting incredibly rapidly. Indeed, many digital platforms and tools (Twitter, Snapchat, e-courses, Pinterest) are designed to give us as many images and nuggets of information as quickly and seductively as possible. It's soothing to, for example, scroll through images of homes decorated for a holiday on Pinterest: the images are endless, and they wash over us. It's empowering (in a sense) to scroll through our newsfeed on Twitter, "liking" and retweeting, sharing with outrage and a sense of purpose.

Our emotions, hungers, hopes, and fears are being activated. The yawning sense of "I want/I need/I should" is activated, but not in a way that can lead to a healthy outcome: education, study, reflection, time for pause, time for connection, conversation, sustenance.

For these reasons, when we encounter something violent or disturbing online, we are not in the practice of pausing. Our choices seem to be: defriend or block the offending person, immediately type out a response that either solidifies our own position as expert or "the right one" or undermines the other person's point of view or credibility, or ignore, delete, or retreat.

When we feel overwhelmed at the types of conversation we're seeing, we may find that sharing humorous or inspiring quotes or videos is helpful, or we may vigorously "like" and re-share images and statements that take down the points of view of those with whom we disagree. All of this happens very rapidly: click, share, like, retweet, delete, block. In early 2017, in Los Angeles, March mid-term elections were held. Measures on the ballot included issues on raising or lowering taxes and addressing homelessness, roads, bicycle lanes, and health care. As local politicians and organizers pointed out, these issues arguably affect Angelenos' lives to a greater degree than which president won national election. And yet, in Los Angeles County, only 11 percent of registered voters turned out to vote.

Why don't we vote? Why isn't the dialogue, debate, and wide array of stormy, inspiring, infuriating, seductive, and creative content with which we so constantly engage online indicative of actual political action? One answer: we don't take time to pause, process, or reflect. Time for reflection has the capacity to transform us, body and mind, but we rarely access this resource. When "time is money" and we glorify "being busy" and multitasking, we suffer—but reflective practice is always available, and can be used immediately by anyone, anywhere. It's our most immediate and underused ingredient for fostering interfaith grit.

Because encounter with difference can be discomfiting and transformative, it is likely that connecting reflective practice to grit will benefit us individually, and also benefit leaders who seek to develop and foster interfaith education and initiatives. This chapter is a starting point for considering how interfaith leaders can best facilitate spaces, methods, and encounters that lead to the kind of personal and community transformation interfaith work makes possible.

What does "interfaith" mean?

Interfaith: For me, religious education seeks to develop methods and techniques for participants to query questions of faith and spirituality, and which then leads to participants growing and becoming transformed.

Thus, it follows that inter-religious education seeks to allow for spaces where participants from different faith traditions (or religious traditions, or from ethical commitments) come together for learning, for dialogue, and for mutual enrichment. For interfaith education to work, it must allow for participants to share their perspectives and wisdom, co-creating meaning and purpose. An inter-religious educator will be a facilitator, shepherd, coach, or co-learner, but will not be teaching content... because the content of inter-religious education comes, by necessity, from and through those engaging in it. We are the content. Our lives are the content. Our fears, children, parents, tragedies, hopes, and similarities are the content.

It is also important to define key terms that I use throughout: "inter-religious," "inter-religious education," and "interfaith." In this book, "inter-religious" refers to a conversation or space shared by multiple dialogue partners. That is, within the conversation, lesson, experience, or encounter, participants name and can be known by their religious or ethical tradition, and this religion or ethical tradition can inform their participation in the space.

Participation is key. This kind of learning cannot be passive. Imagine the difference between watching a cooking show and attempting to make ravioli from scratch the first time. Watching passively, you may appreciate both how beautiful and difficult it is to stretch, fill, and form the pasta. But when actually doing it—you are learning the texture of the dough, the nuanced difference between rolling just thin enough and the dough breaking, the scent and heat of the filling, the pleasing way the edges crimp with the fork, and the disappointment when poorly formed ones break in water. While making them, you might be experiencing memories about eating canned ravioli as a child with cousins, or fantasies you had about having parents who cooked, or new ideas about traveling to Italy with a lover. You may experience frustration with your thick, unyielding fingers, and embarrassment that you have never been able to afford good cookware, and impatience with your significant other who doesn't want to help.

In passive learning, some parts of our brains, hearts, and bodies are activated.

In participatory learning, so many more parts of your brain, body, memory, emotions, and abilities to collaborate, problem solve, balance, and *build up your capacity to make mistakes and keep trying.*

In addition, when we partake of participatory learning *with others*, all of these capacities and strengths are magnified. It can be frightening—or exhilarating!—to try new things, make mistakes, and learn about ourselves in front of others. And yet, the relationships that are built, and the self-knowledge that we gain from learning with others—these positive outcomes strengthen all points of learning, especially learning in diverse contexts.

There are some problems with multiculturalism and religious education. I use "inter-religious education," as distinct from "religious education" or "multicultural education." In the latter, differences are named and valued, but religious, faith, or ethical commitments are not necessarily made explicit or leveraged. Often, in multiculturalism, we highlight, share, celebrate, and work to tolerate differences. The differences we choose to highlight are often surface-level differences, and can often make outsiders to various traditions mistakenly believe they are monolithic.

For example, in the month of December, well-meaning teachers and religious leaders often share Christmas and Hanukkah side by side, as key examples from two Abrahamic traditions, and in hopes of being inclusive. And that's a great start! However, Christmas is one of two *major*, foundational holidays in Christianity. It represents one of two key beliefs (that God found a way to be born as a human into our world). (The other key belief is that Jesus died and came back to life, celebrated in Easter.) But Hanukkah is a "lesser feast" in Judaism—key holidays in Judaism are Rosh Hashanah and Yom Kippur. It is good to know about Hanukkah, and very good to make space in our inclusive holiday lives to learn about it and celebrate it, but years of seeing Christmas and Hanukkah highlighted side by side has given many Americans the false impression that they are equal in some way. Worse, this false equivalency has given many Americans the sense that they know something important about Judaism, and so they don't need to learn much else.

In "religious education," either the educator or material is mono-religious or ecumenical, or the starting place or frameworks come from Christian religious education. In contrast, "inter-religious education" seeks to have multiple voices as "teachers," a diverse body of learners, and attempts to bring into the educational space—either by material or through facilitation—time and space for learning *about* religious difference and for learning *how to learn or live with* religious difference. Religious education is still important—we must know about ourselves, and about our own histories, and the lineage of readings, actions, and communities that precede us and ground our existence. And yet: if we are going to participate in diverse communities and be open to change, we need to grow beyond mere religious education. We need to encourage and enable others to come with us, as well.

In this way, we're not talking about the kind of theological learning that happens at church or synagogue, or where we learn mostly about our tradition and what other traditions believe. This work is relational. And scary. In traditional coffee hours, adult education programs, lecture series, or book clubs, we explore ideas, but we explore ideas with people who are like us. We might gain new information, or appreciate new viewpoints, but we aren't often challenged to the point of feeling uncomfortable.

If we never feel uncomfortable, how can we be changed? The central thesis of this book is that uncertainty and disequilibrium have the potential to crack us open and propel us into positive transformation. As C. S. Lewis said, "You cannot go on indefinitely being just an ordinary, decent egg. We must be hatched or go bad." How do we hatch? And how, as leaders, do we help our communities not fear hatching? It takes grit.

This book is the culmination of formal research with interfaith teachers in higher education, over ten years of experience teaching in and learning from religiously and culturally diverse communities, encounters with curious kindred spirits in countries including Haiti, India, and the Czech Republic, and ongoing engagement with storytelling as a reflective, transformative practice. You will find it useful in understanding why we humans resist difference, and how (paradoxically!) exposure to difference—and embrace of the other—can gild our lives with meaning and richness.

The Problem
Our World Just Won't Stay Still

Babies and toddlers are used to their worlds being upended. Depth perception, object permanence, new textures and foods—reality shifts, is added to and changed; new information transforms what they thought they knew, all day long.

Dissonance is uncomfortable. We are literally experiencing a shakiness which can feel like a threat to the world, and how we fit in it. And yet, disequilibrium precedes all real learning. It's a necessary ingredient to learning. If we hope to learn, if we seek to mature, we must take the risk of being changed.

How do we cope with change? How do we cope with difference? Some of us avoid. Some flee. Some bargain, and some try to debate. Some experience a crisis of faith or become paralyzed by moral relativism. Some fear outsiders as a perceived threat. Some become energized by travel, new foods, new customs, and difference. Some meet great friends, roommates, coworkers, or fall in love with someone different. Some feel their own religious or ethical traditions illuminated or strengthened by exposure to and relationship with difference.

What divides these two groups of people? Or rather, what keeps us from being more open to difference? Are some of us more naturally inclined be okay with this dissonance? Are there practices or things we can learn to help us deal with disequilibrium? Can we teach those in our communities to encounter difference with a positive posture of openness?

This book operates on the idea that we can become more comfortable with difference. Further, if we are a teacher, parent, religious leader, or manager in a workplace or organization, it is our responsibility to help others grow in their ability to withstand dissonance. It takes a little courage, it takes a willingness to be occasionally uncomfortable—it takes interfaith grit.

Recently, there has been a bit of a backlash against the idea of "grit," especially as applied to urban youth—the concept has been much in public discussion. But misconceptions about grit and resilience characterize those traits as somehow innate. In fact, resilience is a transferable skill. It is a practice, and leaders can help teach and foster strategies that lead to great resilience and, in turn, to more effective learning and lasting positive relationships.[1]

What do we know about resiliency, psychology, and the human brain? The work of Norman Garmezy has been instrumental in the development of the study of human resiliency as a field. The literature begins in child psychology and psychiatry in the 1960s and 1970s on "vulnerable children," "social effectiveness," "protective factors," "temperament," and "social competence," including the work of Norman Garmezy, Edward Zigler, Ann Masten, Michael Rutter, and Leslie Phillips. Moving into the 1980s and 1990s, research covered such concepts as "stress resistant," "risk," "vulnerability," "coping," and "adjustment," with the work of the authors mentioned above, as well as J. K. Felsman, Eric Dubow, A. L. Rabin, and J. Aronoff. Resiliency emerged as a concept that could be studied and applied in education.

As early as the 1970s, Garmezy and Masten were identifying examples of "at risk" children who succeeded despite their circumstances. Garmezy in particular sought to lead a shift in researching moving from how to protect children in troubled circumstances to trying to understand how children who thrived anyway did so.

---

1. See Brooks, "Putting Grit in Its Place." For a recent recap of the body of popular literature, see also Tough, "How Kids Learn Resilience."

By 2006, developmental psychologists and educators had made that transition; the new perspective is exemplified with Steven J. Condly (summing the work of Garmezy, Masten, and their peers in "Resilience in Children: A Review of Literature with Implications for Education") writes,

> There is a clear class of children who defy the conventional wisdom and not only survive hostile environments but also actually thrive; these are the resilient . . . resilience is . . . perceived as a label that defines the interaction of a child with trauma or a toxic environment in which success . . . is achieved by virtue of the child's abilities, motivations, and support systems.[2]

Over the course of shifting from looking at children who weren't thriving, to seeking to understand the special capacities that thriving children had, terms such as "invulnerability," "adaptation," and "competence" were used by researchers.

The idea of "competence" as a positive attribute to be studied exemplifies the switch to studying positive capacities in children instead of keeping track of the trauma surrounding them. Ann Masten, herself a pioneer in this area, tracks the development of the field in "Resilience in Developmental Psychopathology: Contributions of the Project Competence Longitudinal Study," written in 2012. Masten writes, "To investigate resilience, we defined and measured the quality of adaptive behavior . . . the nature and severity of adversity or risk encountered, and the individual or contextual differences that might account for the variable patterns of adaptation."[3] Note that current resilience research still focuses on the behaviors and capacities of individual children—developmental psychologists have made recommendations to parents and teachers, but teachers have not made links between what makes up resilience and what can be taught or fostered at school. A current scan of the field of resilience in education reveals studies for teachers *about* resilience and programs that can build resilience in

---

2. Condly, "Resilience in Children," 211–36.
3. Masten and Tellegen, "Resilience in Developmental Psychopathology," 345–61.

at-risk youth, but there is no mention of how resilience and inter-religious education may be linked, or how they can benefit from one another. Currently we know a great deal about resilient children and even about the resources that sustain them. Next steps for widening the field will include broadening our understanding of resilience in adult populations, linking resilience to specific areas, like inter-religious education, and learning how such connections cause learning to flourish (or not).

In this section, we will briefly examine key features of resiliency as it has been applied in developmental psychology and education, with particular attention to the latter. This research seeks to explore if and how resiliency might be an essential ingredient for inter-religious education. To that end, we will connect aspects of resilience that are particularly integral to inter-religious learning.

In 1970, the father of resiliency research, Norman Garmezy, presented a paper entitled "Vulnerability Research and the Issue of Primary Prevention" at the annual meeting of the American Orthopsychiatric[4] Association. By "primary prevention," Garmezy means "coping," and he sought to understand how some young people—even with few resources—coped with stress and trauma better than others. This was a puzzle; researchers were seeking to learn why some children succeeded against all odds. Could they learn from those "high risk" children? As Garmezy put it, "a simple declaration of physical, psychosocial or sociocultural resources cannot explain divergent paths to adaptation or to deviance."[5] This "variability in outcomes"[6] led to Garmezy's consideration of development from the end (either the traumatized and not flourishing, or traumatized and *still* flourishing) child, to try and determine what had justified that outcome. This was a new lens with which to consider the outcome—previously, researchers (including

---

4. Orthopsychiatry is the study of mental or developmental disorders, with particular emphasis on children and child development. This field is now known as child and adolescent psychiatry.

5. Garmezy, "Vulnerability Research and the Issue of Primary Prevention," 106.

6. Ibid.

Garmezy) had begun with the starting situation or traumas (poverty, illness, sick mother, low IQ). Garmezy marks this new lens and the meaning for how researchers saw children within the context of his outcomes as he writes,

> Provide us with a slum child who is forging a pattern of strength and we will cast about for environmental surrogates who *must* have served as inoculators against despair, for events that *must* have encouraged hope rather than hopelessness, for inner resources that *must* have proclaimed vitality rather than helplessness. However, were we to convert this same slum child into someone prone to violence or aberration, our focus would be turned with equal efficiency and perhaps even greater facility to alternate figures and facets that would buttress our perception of deviance.[7]

Note that even Garmezy's verb "inoculate" suggests the idea that something external, when applied to a child, can foster healing and strength. Instead, what Garmezy and his peers find is that the strength is already present within some children and adults.

How does this relate to possibilities for inter-religious education? When we examine engagement in inter-religious settings, we will find that some participants are able to withstand the disruption and dissonance of alterity better than others. And yet, learning cannot take place if participants abandon the project as soon as they feel uncomfortable. One task of inter-religious educators and facilitators is to create containers and methods to foster a kind of in-the-moment resiliency in students, so that they might draw upon interior and even external resources (their relationship with peers, support from the instructor, the required nature of a course as extrinsic motivation) to remain participants.

Just as reflective practice ought to be the focus of educational activities, especially in inter-religious settings, so too can resilience be included in models and practices that can be taught and fostered. Although Garmezy made this move in 1970, it is still infrequently included in stated capacities for inter-religious

---

7. Ibid. Emphasis original.

learning, or even religious or multi-cultural learning. Garmezy's early questions provide some ideas for qualities we can examine in this project. He writes,

> Can we use our schools and clinics as centers for training these [high-risk] children in more adaptive techniques for coping? Can we use participation in successful play to increase the flexibility of the response repertoires of these children? Can we stimulate adaptive behavior by introducing into such training centers healthy children who can serve as models for the vulnerable child?[8]

We might well ask the following questions: Can we use our spaces of inter-religious encounter as centers for training students in more adaptive techniques for prolonged engagement with others? Can we use participation in study groups and microteaching to increase the flexibility of response repertoires of these students? Can we stimulate practice in withstanding disruption by introducing models for successful relationship and engagement?

In this chapter, we will explore major themes in resilience research and discover which features might be salient for religious-and inter-religious education. All three strands of our understanding of resilience—competence, coping, and community—offer something that we might glean for inter-religious education.

Even after Garmezy made the initial move from focusing on the negative to examining what might "inoculate" some children against trauma, researchers still tracked the negative attributes of children's surroundings and circumstances. However, once researchers moved to considering the development of "competence," some positive attributes came into focus. Ingrid Schoon, in her book *Risk and Resilience: Adaptations in Changing Times*, identifies the pitfall in focusing on the negative, and demonstrates how far the field had come by 2006. Schoon argues, "A focus on resilience and resources, on the other hand, aims to understand adaptive development in spite of risk exposure and to maximise [sic] wellness even before maladjustment has occurred,"[9] and underscores her

---

8. Ibid, 114.
9. Schoon, *Risk and Resilience*, 158.

point, writing, "the resilience framework entails emphasis not on deficits but on areas of strength."[10] As we shall see, once researchers began considering areas of strength as well as deficit, and examined "understanding adaptive development" as part of a wider interpersonal matrix, the field began to include capacities that can be isolated, taught, developed, and modeled in interfaith settings.

By the early 1980s, some developmental psychologists began to tease out the meaning of "competence" or "social competence" as related but separate from resilience. In "Social Competence as a Developmental Construct," Everett Waters and L. Alan Sroufe define competence in a way particularly suited to our purposes. That is, they move from considering a person's interior resources to thinking about what a person *does*. This action focus is helpful as we consider which capacities can be taught and fostered. Waters and Sroufe write, "Competence is viewed as an integrative concept which refers broadly to an *ability to generate and coordinate flexible, adaptive responses to demands and to generate and capitalize on opportunities in the environment* (i.e., effectiveness)."[11] Competence in this form is easier to measure as a competency. That is, we can look for evidence of inner resilience, but it seems difficult to articulate as a learning outcome. In contrast, competence per Waters's and Sroufe's definition points us to looking for responses to concrete moments. One can imagine, in an interfaith setting, creating a microteaching opportunity to engage in a disruptive idea—the use of case studies comes to mind as one potential example. After the initial lesson, time for reflection can be expanded to include questions like, "What was your initial impression?"; "What was your process for working through the dilemma?"; "Did your ideas change during the encounter?"; and "What resources (prior experiences or knowledge, modelling by instructor or peers, relationship) helped you work through the experience?"

We notice that these are questions of reflection; indeed, the reflection and resilience are related. If we consider reflection to be

---

10. Ibid., 160.

11. Waters and Sroufe, "Social Competence as a Developmental Construct," 80. Emphasis original.

a flexible, responsive action-in-practice, this concept meets another part of Waters's and Sroufe's articulation of competence. They continue, writing, "Competence . . . *is identified with the ability to mobilize and coordinate these resources in such a way that opportunities are created and the potentials or resources in the environment are realized; again, for a good developmental outcome.*"[12] This idea of "coordination" reminds us of metaphors used to describe artists or jazz musicians. In addition, coordination itself is a practice. That is, students can identify the components of coordination (identifying resources, applying ideas, evaluating their success, reflecting on the outcome), practice them, and share their practice with others.

Coordination is also a positive attribute (in the sense that it is a skill one possesses, unlike precursor ideas of resiliency that sought to describe how a person should have been failing to thrive, given the conditions surrounding them) in addition to being a practice. In "IQ and Ego-Resiliency: Conceptual and Empirical Connections and Separateness," Jack Block and Adam M. Kremen note both that competence is a practice and that it is also rooted in outward engagement with others. First, Block and Kremen write, "Within a single life, too, it will be observed that at times a person is much more resourceful and adaptively effective than at other times."[13] With this in mind, we move from the idea of "an invulnerable person" whose resilience allows her to overcome all manner of obstacles to the sense that all of us are more or less resourceful and adaptive at different points. This is good news for those of us who would seek to develop resilience as a capacity in education. Similarly, we find another part of the capacity that can be taught in Block and Kreman's connection between resilience and engagement. They write, "ego-resilience is expected to predispose individuals not only to an absence of susceptibility to anxiety but also to a positive engagement with the world, as manifested by positive affect and openness to experience."[14] And here again is a practice;

12. Ibid., 83. Emphasis original.
13. Block and Kreman, "IQ and Ego-Resiliency," 349.
14. Ibid., 351.

The Problem

learners can practice a posture of openness to experience. This also can be deliberately included in direct instruction and modelling in inter-religious classes and settings. Below, we shall explore more deeply how "positive engagement with the world" supports a kind of resilience that might support deeper and longer-lasting student engagement.

Longer-lasting engagement with the materials, settings, and encounters of inter-religious education is necessary because inter-religious learning requires movement, over time, through several ways of being; this theory of development is described both formally by inter-religious scholar educators and by voices in our participant interviews. For example, imagine the time involved in practicing and becoming more masterful at the kinds of learning Judith Berling describes, writing, "Learning in a diverse world requires not merely mastering some set of information but also learning to understand and negotiate areas of human difference, envisioning new ways of being and new possibilities."[15] To learn how interfaith education actually happened—and to identify best practices—I interviewed ten practitioners in higher education settings across the United States. I asked them to reflect upon the qualities they saw in themselves and their students, and to describe interfaith learning at its best. While at least one interview participant noted that, at some level, her role does require her to give students enough new information—particularly about new traditions or religions—mastering mere information takes some time. Learning to understand difference can be for many of us a life-long practice, and becoming visionary in the way one regards conflict and possibilities may rarely be possible in academic time parcels.

In fact, each one of these categories of learning can be broken apart into smaller tasks or realizations that inter-religious educators try to facilitate. F. is a Jewish professor of religion in both a rabbinical school and a large public university; he also serves on several large inter-religious non-profits and facilitates Jewish-Christian and Jewish-Muslim adult educational events. F. describes the kind of beginning reflective work that students and

15. Berling, *Understanding Other Religious Worlds*, 26.

participants often encounter earlier in their learning processes. He began by asserting that initial introductory knowledge about other traditions should lead to more substantial developments. When asked about the outcomes of one of his classes, he began by stating,

> A student is able to—there are a couple of different levels I think—the student is able to be literate in some of the concepts, practices, and language and vocabulary of the other religious traditions (and we are talking only about three and that is, right? We are talking about Islam, Christianity, and Judaism.) So people, everyone who leaves the class has to know, because I ask them on a quiz, on a midterm or a final what—they have to know the words "Surah" and "Hadith" and "Ayat" and what this "Quran" actually means.
>
> What does "Islam" mean? And I don't—these are just real basics, but they have to know that, same thing about "Torah," "Talmud," stuff like that. It is a little bit less problematic in the Christian world because we live in such a Christianized culture, that kind of vocabulary and assumption is there.
>
> So there is that—another outcome is a, I think, is a deeper respect for a scripture and [the] religious sensibilities of another religious, at least two other religious communities with the expectation of the hope that transfers beyond . . . creates a kind of attitudinal development.[16]

After a pause, F. moved to describing a kind of "learning to negotiate human difference" continuing,

> And flexibility in thinking that is really important, we spend a lot of time on reading, what is the reading process, when we read things, not just words on a page but when we read people, when we read people's clothing, when we read architecture, how are we actually processing the information that we are getting, how much are we looking objectively of the material and to what extent are we inserting our own history into our processing, all of

---

16. F., in discussion with the author, October 2014.

that is really, we are very content about that, we are very, what is the word for it?[17]

F. was encouraged with a question prompting, "But it's deliberate," and F. affirmed, "Deliberate, we are deliberate."[18] When asked about challenges to students making that move from learning content to learning practice, he answered,

> I think the overwhelming one is getting beyond the—, and [then to] acknowledge stereotypes, I think that is the issue because it creates, I think, real barriers from the very beginning that people aren't really aware of, it's a kind of preconceived notion, prejudices, pre-judgments that we have that we are really unaware of . . . They are not intentional—that color our ability to see the phenomenon that we are looking at in a way that is, I don't want to use the word "positive" but in a way that is more real, right.
>
> Or a way that that phenomenon is associated with something, a phenomenon that is associated with, let's say religion or culture—where the observer sees it in the way the presenter would like it to be seen or sees it himself or herself.[19]

By identifying the ability of a learner to see from her co-learner's point of view, F. echoes here classic foreparents of inter-religious dialogue, including Raimon Pannikar, Wilfred Cantwell Smith, and Leonard Swidler; interfaith theologian Judith Berling also captures this interpretive process when she declares,

> Unraveling, naming, and describing the threads of the learning process offer an interpretation of that process. The five threads are 1) encountering difference or entering another world; 2) one's initial response . . . ;[20] 3)

---

17. Ibid.
18. Ibid.
19. Ibid.
20. Berling's original phrasing is, "one's initial response as a Christian," but nothing in this research indicates that it matters which religion or tradition is the starting place in this process.

conversation and dialogue on several levels; 4) living out what has been learned; and 5) internalizing the process.[21]

Again, we see that what can be phrased succinctly can take years of practice and engagement. For those who see inter-religious dialogue as personally spiritually enriching (for example, à la Paul Knitter's *Without Buddha I Could Not Be a Christian*, or countless mono-religious adult education earnest endeavors to understand neighbors), part of the reason spiritual development happens is that inter-religious encounter can take time—giving reflective practice time a chance to connect to spiritual and emotional practices, new habits, the time to take chances and try new ways of engaging, and time to build relationships. In the next section, relationship building particularly will be related to resilience; let us keep in mind that relationships also take time to build, another reason resilience to withstand new encounters is beneficial for longer-lasting inter-religious engagement.

Ingrid Schoon explores the idea of "adaptation" as a key part of resilience in her *Risk and Resilience: Adaptations in Changing Times*. Schoon is more interested in the "ordinary[22] adaptive processes"[23] as a dynamic, ongoing process than in what might inoculate an individual from the impact of her surroundings. For Schoon, adaptation is part of a life-long process and individuals are intimately connected through their relationships with others; both of these influence how and why one might be resilient in a given situation. As we review Schoon's emphasis on interconnectedness and the dynamic construction of life course, let us keep in mind possible features that might be mapped onto inter-religious education.

Schoon articulates five principles as part of the concept of "life-course" in competency; she enumerates the following:

---

21. Berling, *Understanding Other Religious Worlds*, 2.

22. Schoon riffs on "ordinary" from Ann S. Masten's 2001 assertion that resilience is but an "ordinary magic" in the latter's *American Psychologist* article of the same name.

23. Schoon, *Risk and Resilience*, 12.

1. Human development is a life-long process.

2. Individuals construct their own life course through choices and actions they take within the opportunities and constraints of history and social circumstances, a principle also referred to as human agency.

3. The life course is embedded and shaped by social structures and the historical times and places experienced by individuals over their lifetime.

4. The developmental antecedents and consequences of life transitions, events and behaviour [sic] patterns vary according to their timing in a person's life.

5. Lives are lived interdependently, and social and historical influences bear on this network of linked lives.[24]

While these concepts are connected to resilience as understood by Garmezy, for example, we see that Schoon has definitively moved beyond thinking about flaws that need to be addressed, or disordered individuals that might be studied. Instead, she has moved into considering interdependent relationships and how these "networks of shared relationships"[25] surround individual development. As Schoon puts it, "resilience is a multidimensional phenomenon."[26] All five of Schoon's life-course aspects coordinate with the work of educators, and can be included in inter-religious pedagogy. Indeed, Schoon takes a kind of holistic approach to understanding how and when individuals are resilient, and how they can both learn from their own experiences and help teach others in their "network of linked lives." This is the stuff of both religious education and inter-religious education. Is it possible to leverage this network to foster resilient practices? Are religious or inter-religious communities particularly suited to cultivating positive networks for this growth?

---

24. Ibid., 23–24.
25. Ibid., 31.
26. Ibid., 147.

Pioneers in the area of resilience research barely mention religion as a factor in resilience. Occasionally, one will note that "religiousness" can provide an external resource for those suffering from illness or trauma, but it has been left relatively unexplored, particularly when compared to the field as a whole. In "Anchored by Faith: Religion as a Resilience Factor," by Kenneth I. Pargament and Jeremy Cummings, the obstacles faced by those wishing to include religion are described in their survey of human resilience. They write,

> In spite of the fact that the founding figures in psychology viewed religion as central to an understanding of human behavior, the field of psychology largely neglected religious issues for much of the 20th century. When religion was considered, it was often (1) viewed as a source of pathology, (2) measured by a few global religious items, and (3) explained in terms of purportedly more basic phenomena . . . The number of studies on religion has grown, and it has become clear through this research that religiousness can play a significant role in response to major life stressors.[27]

Pargament and Cummings assert "religiousness is a significant resilience factor for many people."[28] Pargament in particular has done much of the foundational research connecting religiousness and resilience, and he bemoans the fact that researchers have "neglected or diminished"[29] the role of religion to this point. For a religious educator or practical theologian, though, Pargament and Cummings cover no new ground. They sum how prayer and membership in a religious community give comfort and even pain relief to the afflicted, can give a sense of meaning in the face of trauma, and they explain how some therapists (their examples are all Christian) use "psychospiritual interventions" to enhance their work with patients.[30] Their final assertion, "religiousness can

---

27. Pargament and Cummings, "Anchored by Faith," 193.
28. Ibid., 193.
29. Ibid., 207.
30. For example, clients with an exaggerated sense of suffering can be

be a catalyst for positive life changes and stress-related growth,"[31] is true enough, but they provide no road map for how religious or inter-religious educators might connect religious or ethical commitments and fostering resilience as a capacity for learning.

While reflective practice includes competencies that dovetail well with religious and inter-religious education, resilience as a possible competency fits less well. Limitations include: focus on the personal, to the exclusion of considering how resilience might be fostered in group settings like classrooms; focus on internal processes; and lack of research on how people might learn resilience practices.

And yet, challenges in life—and in the classroom—are normal, particularly when we move beyond shallow, more initial relationships and experiences into the turbulence that truer encounters can create. As we close this section, let us examine some possible connections between competence or resilience and the wider learning community that surrounds individuals. These connections are most likely to be fruitful for understanding how resilience might work as a capacity in inter-religious learning.

Masten and J. Douglas Coatsworth, writing in 1998, echo the emergence of "competence" as a key, related concept as well as the addition of context and community as important factors in an individual's resilience. In "The Development of Competence in Favorable and Unfavorable Environments: Lessons From Research on Successful Children," they note, "[Competence] refers to good adaptation and not necessarily to superb achievement,"[32] and " . . . the two most widely reported predictors of resilience appear to be relationships with caring prosocial adults and good intellectual functioning."[33] This makes sense: not only that relationships can

---

reminded that the crucifixion was "particularly terrible" and yet Jesus did not attempt to escape it.

31. Pargament and Cummings, "Anchored by Faith," 193.

32. Masten and Coatsworth, "The Development of Competence in Favorable and Unfavorable Environments," 206.

33. Ibid., 212.

support individual, interior resilience, but perhaps that relationships and community create spaces where resilience-building practices can be worked out. *If adaptation and the importance of relationship are linked, we can perhaps expand possibilities for resilience practice in community.*

Monique Boekaerts explores coping and personal and academic goals, and seeks to understand how teachers might facilitate growth in coping behaviors. Boekaerts carefully examines examples of "stressors" for students, and recommends ways teachers can foster "metacognitive knowledge"[34] that will allow students to recognize the processes at work in encountering adversity and overcoming it. In our global, fractious communities, metacognition will also enable us to take a step back and reconsider expansive possibilities, worldviews, and possible responses. Boekaerts writes, "I do not deny that a stressor causes a state of imbalance or incongruence in the information processing system, but I believe that the present coping models do not adequately address *intentionality*."[35] She seeks to articulate "adequate coping models"[36] and encourages teachers to consider including them in their repertoire of models and strategies for fostering reflection in students. She focuses on students' interior lives, highlighting how reflection connects to resilience. She writes,

> I [propose] that successful adaptation to stressful episodes, particularly in transition periods, requires students to achieve a fit between changing physical and social environments and their internal environment. The internal environment includes the students' perception of self, their goal structure, values, motives, and beliefs, but also their capacity to represent a stressor mentally and their ability to select from the repertoire of coping scripts those that best fit their coping goal, given the perceived situational demands.[37]

34. Boekaerts, "Coping in Context," 187.
35. Ibid., 175. Emphasis original.
36. Ibid., 176.
37. Ibid.

Given the positive, supporting benefits of prosocial relationships with others, it makes sense that sharing "coping scripts" might be a way for students to learn from one another and practice additional ways of coping. There are other possibilities for rich practice here. "Perceived situational demands" can be helped with the appliation of self-reflection and by considering new possibilities to meet these demands. For example, we can imagine the use of narrative pedagogy as one way to help surface new possibilities for consideration. As Boekaerts puts it,

> The outcome of this reflection process [on the source of the difficulty and the amount of effort needed to solve the problem] is the choice of a coping strategy. When these students consider it meaningful to invest resources, they will continue striving, investing effort to adapt the plan so that it fits local conditions.[38]

The idea that meaning outweighs stress could be especially constructive when considering how to frame the dissonance that arises in interfaith encounters. Educators can capitalize on the intrinsic investment of effort students bring to experiences they consider meaningful and meet them with practices that make students' coping most beneficial. One can imagine, for example, the inclusion of "encountering and solving disruptive puzzles" in inter-religious courses or programs. Facilitators could name and make explicit some common reactions, as well as coach practice sessions (microteaching or micropractice) where students articulate their processes and share with one another.

Boekaerts also suggests the kind of questions facilitators might use. While she is thinking particularly of "stressors" and "coping goals," we can imagine the usefulness of such facilitation in inter-religious education settings. Boekaerts writes,

> Teachers should be given training in raising and answering a set of associated questions. These include: What are the objective characteristics of this stressor?; Did you interpret the stressor correctly?; What is your

---

38. Ibid., 187.

coping goal?; Did you select a coping strategy in accordance with your coping goal? These and similar questions may help students to think about their coping attempts and to explore different coping responses and their effect. In addition, students may be willing to compare and contrast their own coping strategies with those of peers. Coping strategies that others use and prove to be effective in a particular context, yet do not violate the students' personal values (higher order goals), may swiftly be incorporated into his or her coping repertoire, whereas strategies that are deemed effective by somebody else, but prove to be cumbersome, embarrassing, or unacceptable, may be foregone.[39]

Boekaerts's description of how a teacher might facilitate reflection and sharing of strategies fits well in religious education settings, and aligns reflective practice with resilience. And so, we've come full circle, beginning with reflective practice, moving across the historical development of the field of resilience research, and beginning to consider how the two areas might work together in inter-religious education settings.

In her seminal work, Berling teaches us how to foster conflict fluency, which means having the capacity to:

- anticipate a range of possible scenarios about how our future relationships will evolve in unfamiliar cultural contexts
- remain conscious of unfamiliar cultural influences that come to be embedded in our meaning-making processes
- express what is deep down in our cultural assumptions, in a way that is understandable to others unfamiliar with our meaning-making patterns
- navigate the turbulence of cross-cultural dynamics in order to co-create a constructive future together with cultural others.

Before we can navigate turbulence, we must go willingly there. It does no good to practice comfort with difference if we

---

39. Ibid., 194.

The Problem

remain in our comfort zones. Knowing that all adults naturally resist this, what practices can we model, foster, require, and assess?

Exposure to difference can exist on a spectrum. Consider the following opportunities:

- Eat vegetarian, eat vegan, eat Jain vegan
- Buy groceries from a market you'd usually never enter
- Buy a gift in a shop where you're uncomfortable: a tattoo shop, a luxury spa, an occult bookstore, a motorcycle shop, a pipe store, a pawn shop, a botánica, a Catholic gift shop
- Observe your religion with a group from another ethnicity; go more than once
- Listen to news radio on a station that holds different viewpoints than yours
- Join a Facebook group or follow on Twitter parents that you disagree with (on vaccination, on corporal punishment, on food and nutrition, on schooling)

Resist the need to be right. Resist the desire to debate. Resist rolling your eyes, disparaging, or ranting. If you find yourself imagining how you'd convince them of your point of view, take a deep breath and remember tools that aid grit: reflection and relationship. Pause, and take time to reflect. Or build and lean upon relationships with those who are different than you (childhood friends, cousins, parents of your children's friends, colleagues, neighbors.) Focus on what you have in common, what you appreciate, and where you feel appreciated. Remind yourself of the richness and value that embracing difference can have for your intellectual, emotional, and spiritual life.

In a church setting, you might consider the following:

- Change the style of seating, of music
- Invite speakers who are normally not represented in the pulpit: women, children, the aged, those with disabilities, those who do not speak the dominant language well, those who cannot read

- In a worship setting, use text instead of spoken word, or remove text entirely
- Invite the marginalized (the homeless, immigrants, formerly incarcerated, teenagers) to sit in positions usually set aside for those with power
- Make sure you build in time for reflection: This will be upsetting for most in the congregation, and so time for pause, pain, discussion, reflection, and dialogue are necessary. Prepare for anger, for confusion, distrust, uneasy laughter, accusations, threats, fear, and anxiety.

Michelle LeBaron's work in family law, conflict resolution, and mediating seemingly intractable cultural conflict gives us useful resources for framing our own practices and entrenched worldviews. In her seminal work, *Bridging Cultural Conflicts: A New Approach for a Changing World*, she includes reminders to approach our own values and beliefs with the same curiosity and flexibility as we do those of strangers. Her questions include:

- Why do you hold this belief or view?
- Where does it come from?
- How does this belief influence you and your life?
- Now, assume the completely opposite view to the one you hold. What is it?
- How does it make sense for those who hold this view?
- What can you imagine might reinforce this view for those who hold it?
- With this alternate belief, what would your world look and feel like now?

How can you and your communities live out radical perspective taking practices? How often do you take the opportunity to meet others in their religious worlds?

What do we mean when we decide we should try to understand other religious worlds? In 2004, Berling wrote

Understanding Other Religious Worlds: A Guide for Interreligious Education. In it, she traces her own trajectory in understanding the need for her teaching to become mindful of inter-religious differences. Berling was first interested in theology, and then comparative theology. She noticed that her own interest in helping her students become responsible, curious explorers made her more interested in creating a "guide" for this kind of exploration. She details what learning other religions should entail, and delineates the kinds of assignments and processes that support inter-religious education. My understanding of "inter-religious education" closely mirrors hers.

Berling begins by noting the need for openness to difference, writing, "A learner's tentative and initial understanding of a religion *must be subject to correction* by the specific texts, terms, and distinctive perspectives of the religion. That requires attention to and respect for difference."[40]

Berling is describing the knowledge and provisional understandings that learners bring with them. What do you bring with you to an encounter? How long have you carried these texts and tentative understandings?

Examples of "texts" might include: songs from Girl or Boy Scouts, childhood television shows and movies, holiday traditions, beliefs or practices about food and cooking, scary stories we learned as children, worries about what women and men can and can't do, the magazines we read, the places where we vacation and what we experience there, and our communities' beliefs and practices around playing outside, voting and participating in public service, sharing public space, noise, and art. We have all of this artful baggage we carry around inside, and this helps us answer the question, "How does the world work?"

Take a moment to think about that. When you consider this question, what kinds of images or ideas flash through your mind? Do you picture God as a white man with a long beard, setting our lives in motion like we are playthings? Do you picture "family" as a man and a woman, with an ambitious man working

---

40. Berling, *Understanding Other Religious Worlds*, 40. Emphasis mine.

outside the home, and a happy mom making dinner in a warm kitchen? In your ideas about the world, are police officers kindly and helpful, or threatening and dishonest? Does voting matter? Can anyone be president?

If you are an educator or leader in your ethical or religious community, consider helping others in your community through activities to help them understand the artful baggage they carry that informs the way they see the world. Do your religious, ethical, or political institutions help inform those perspectives in a healthy and true way? Or do some of the systems in which you participate obscure or distort certain truths?

Let's look again at Berling's quote about our first understandings: she writes, "A learner's tentative and initial understanding of a religion must be subject to correction by the specific texts, terms, and distinctive perspectives of the religion. That requires attention to and respect for difference."[41]

First, we have to identify and name the first ways we know about the world, the first understandings we've used to make sense of how the world works.

Then—and this is hard—we have to open ourselves to correction. We have to be willing to be wrong. The texts we know and love—our own most beloved artful baggage—might actually be harmful. They might keep us from experiencing the world fully, or from truly engaging with others as we are meant to do.

Note that Berling, as a teacher and as a writer, takes great care to track how we learn. This attention to the learner is central to inter-religious education. Whereas comparative theologians might situate their own confessional natures within their wider research, learning about and comparing other theologies remains central. In contrast, inter-religious education focuses on the individual learner, not just the wider context. The learner as co-meaning maker remains primary to those working in this field.

What is a "co-meaning maker"? From the moment we open our eyes and begin to relate to the world and those around us, we are applying what we experience and learn to create a sense

---

41. Berling, *Understanding Other Religious Worlds*, 40.

of *what the world means*. If our caregivers spend time giving us frequent and sustained eye contact, respond to our cries of hunger and discomfort, and allow us to take risks and feel safe, we learn that the world is safe and full of opportunities to explore in ways that make us feel good and capable.

While comparative theologians definitely benefit from reflecting upon the teaching-learning experience, in inter-religious education as an emerging field, the focus on the learner is primary. Francis X. Clooney, a Jesuit Roman Catholic priest and one of the foreparents of comparative theology, took care to emphasize the discursive pattern of movement—from learning, to communicating—that learners experience. Given this, we can at this point posit that in inter-religious education, *learning will always be followed by an outward turn to others*. Inter-religious education as a field benefits from this but, more importantly, learners in inter-religious education *are* inter-religious learners when they practice this move, articulate it, repeat it, and find themselves (possibly) transformed by the pattern.

The work of transformation, the very practice, will always include learning, followed by an outward turn. Then we look around with new eyes, eyes made fresh by curiosity and self-reflection. What do others say? What do our colleagues believe? How do our neighbors grieve? What do other brides wear? Of all the artful baggage we could potentially carry, how did we pick up the pieces that inform our world? And what else is possible?

Because Berling has named her endeavor in the text "a guide for interreligious education," her guidelines for what this entails are worth citing in full. Berling notes, "Learning other religions in a diverse world entails:

- Building on the diversity of learners' experiences while respecting the internal diversity and multiple perspectives of religions studied.

- Empowering learners by developing voice and agency while also teaching them to respect the voices and agencies of those whom they engage in study.

- Entering other worlds through art, text, or narrative so that learners engage difference and particularity while acknowledging their own and others' social locations.
- Engaging understanding and interpretation of the distinctive ways in which religions represent themselves, and not merely the mastery of ungrounded information.
- Developing linguistic flexibility through a mutually critical conversation that engages the languages of all participants, including those of the religions studied,
- Establishing mutually respectful relationships, learning to stand with others."[42]

Two of these have particular utility for the work we're engaging:

Building on the diversity of learners' experiences while respecting the internal diversity . . . of religions studied. For many of us, we recognize that our own culture or religion is diverse, but we don't have the experience yet to know that others are equally as diverse. For example, I'm a Christian. If I meet someone whose only experience with Christianity is Roman Catholicism, and she asks why I want to be part of a church that won't ordain women, I'll say immediately, "But that's only one kind of Christianity!" And yet, the first time I meet a Jain drinking alcohol in an airport bar, I am astonished. "I thought Jains didn't drink!" I think. As we gain more and more information about other cultures, religions, and traditions, we must constantly be on guard that a little expertise doesn't make us experts. It can be exciting to begin learning about others—we may return from our first trip to Europe and want to tell all our friends about how "they" do things there, or start to engage more frequently in online discussions about race after having a black roommate. And yet, first exposure to difference is only the starting place. Within each category there are infinite practices of ways of engaging.

---

42. Ibid., 47–48.

Empowering learners by developing voice and agency while also teaching them to respect the voices and agencies of those whom they engage in study. One of my beloved teachers, Professor Paul Knitter, used to teach us, "Those with the most power must speak last." For those of us who are teachers and leaders, this is tough! We have expertise, we have passion, we have things to say! And yet, even in the way we plan events, set up a room, invite participants, hang flyers, and participate in dialogue, we are operating from *our* sense of the world, and using what makes us most comfortable.

For example, many college or even workplace ice breakers will use the following kind of prompt: "Share your most embarrassing experience." Or, "Share two truths and a lie," with participants adding in slightly outrageous details to make the game more difficult, and more humorous.

In our Western, North American culture, confession and self-deprecation is usual, and admired. We have had decades of reality television and everyday people and movie stars sharing their tragedies, fears, and even crimes with talk show hosts. If someone admits a failure, we praise them for being honest and open and willing to talk about it. But this is not the case in all cultures. When we set the table for dialogue, who are we excluding?

In 2005—at the same time our comparative theologians and religious educators were creating materials and pedagogy in the new field, and at the same time interfaith organizations were succeeding in widening the circle of participants in interfaith engagement—Tiffany Puett wrote "On Transforming Our World: Critical Pedagogy for Interfaith Education," published in *Cross Currents*. In 2005, Puett describes interfaith education as an "emerging field still working to define itself and the challenges it faces."[43] Puett claims activism as a central agent in the development of inter-religious education, and traces a major example to the 1893 Parliament of the World's Religions. Puett asserts,

> Interfaith education grew out of the interfaith movement, a movement with a progressive, activist agenda. The interfaith movement ostensibly began in 1893

---

43. Puett, "On Transforming Our World."

at the World's Parliament of Religions gathering in Chicago, held as part of the World's Fair. This groundbreaking event was the first time in history that leaders of so-called "Eastern" and "Western" religions had come together for dialogue, seeking a common spiritual foundation for global unity . . . Although the organizers of this event were not able to sustain a formal organization, the World's Parliament led to the eventual formation of interfaith organizations dedicated to fostering understanding and dialogue among people of the world's religions.[44]

Note that two field-building interfaith institutions, the United Religions Initiative (URI) and and Interfaith Youth Core (IFYC), also emerged in international, intentionally religious diverse settings; I agree with Puett that large stages with dedicated, far-reaching participants have helped connect the need for interfaith dialogue and education to its development as a field of study and practice.

In addition to the "seeking of a common spiritual foundation," I believe these participants at the 1893 Parliament modeled an embracing of risk—*they flocked to a space with unknown ramifications, even if they had individual aims and agendas*. And one reason it was so fruitful, with so many strands of scholarship and dialogue still growing out, a hundred years hence, was because participants were able to *access and leverage the unknown, reflect upon difference, and experience transformation*—I see these three categories as essential ingredients in inter-religious education.

Nearly every source I surveyed or skimmed (including journal articles from the 1960s and recent compendia of inter-religious education) mention one of three things as crucial points in the development of inter-religious education in the United States: either the 1893 World Parliament of Religions, the book *Nostra Aetate*, or the September 11th, 2001 attacks on the World Trade Center. Sometimes, they use these events and the immediately surrounding materials as direct source material; frequently,

---

44. Ibid.

writers make mere mention of the phrases, "World Parliament," "*Nostra Aetate*," or "9/11" as shorthand for what has become, for many, the American narrative for interfaith. I believe this shorthand reveals what many would like the American interfaith story to be: early historical commitment to the other, validation of cultural changes, and a peaceful response to extraordinary violence.[45] Of course, since Brexit, the 2016 US Presidential election, refugee crises and movements in Europe—all of these political and social movements have led to more debate than dialogue, and more divisiveness than discovery.

In November 2016, Donald Trump was elected the 45th president of the United States. The months leading up to his election, and the period of time immediately following the beginning of his presidency, were divisive and painful for many Americans. Scholars and popular media alike report that Americans live, read, report, and participate in political processes entirely cut off from one another. Words and ideals like "truth" and "American" have different meanings, and are used for purposes that are often at odds with one another.

What does interfaith look like in a time where religious minorities are under attack, where free speech as a right is uncertain, and where hate speech is on the rise—on the walls of our houses of worship, in public, and on social media?

How would you respond to the following scenarios?

You are a youth minister from a small town in the northeastern United States. One of your former youth is married to a Mexican-American. You notice that on her Facebook page, many people who you know from church and from working with the community are posting hateful, racist, and sexist information.

You work for the county clerk's office in a suburban Texas town. You consider yourself progressive, but try to keep political conversations off of your Facebook, because you play a small role in local politics and want to avoid engaging in debate on social

---

45. At least for the American Christian groups and writers I encounter, "9/11" is often the *beginning* of a story about exploring other cultures and realizing that not all non-Christians are bad.

media. During a recent local election, you see a lot of friends and family members posting information that isn't true, from sources that have been proven false.

You are a public middle school principal in a large town in Southern California. You would never tell anyone, but you voted for Trump. You see too many hard-working parents who can barely afford to keep up—you think it's a shame that the middle class is disappearing, and many of your school funds go to children of undocumented immigrants and people on welfare and various disabilities. People you work with often assume that because you work in public schools, you must be liberal, and say hateful things about the stupidity and racism of Trump supporters.

You are the parent of a high school student, and pride yourself on the fact that you've allowed your children to think for themselves and have privacy in your home. However, recently you've noticed that your daughter has been following and liking Twitter posts from so-called "alt-right" voices. You're worried about what she's reading and thinking, and also about how this looks on her public profile when she applies to colleges in the upcoming year.

It's upsetting to see people we like and love post ideas and sentiments we find hurtful or offensive. Many of us resort to "unfriending," "unfollowing," or "muting" voices that run counter to our beliefs on social media. Many of us experience great anxiety when we think about how to navigate political and religious conversations with extended family at holidays and large gatherings. To avoid conflict, we quietly seethe, we change the subject, we avoid talking about the things that matter most, we practice passive aggression, we quietly snark, or we distract ourselves with food and drink.

And yet, being fully human requires us to be in relationship with many others, and in community with a wide variety of people. Our ability to think critically and creatively, and our capacity to communicate, relate, and function, is hindered if we seek to hear and be near only those most like us.

The Problem

Imagine going to a large museum, filled with hundreds of styles of painting, pottery, sculpture, design, metalwork, glass, and ancient artifacts, from thousands of years and culture.

You don't know a lot about all art, but you do know a great deal about Impressionism. It's your favorite kind of art, you've studied it for years and visited museums around the world with Impressionist works. You know all of the major and minor artists and even understand much of the criticism and art theory connected to these works, even though you are a layperson.

When you arrive at the museum, you walk straight to the museum map, careful not to look up at the glass sculpture filling the entry way, or even at signs advertising a special exhibit. You refuse the offer of headphones for a guided tour of the sculpture garden, even though it's free. Finding the wing with the Impressionists' work, you make a beeline for it, and spend two hours there, looking at every piece. Near each of your favorite paintings, you sit, almost meditating. Every didactic calls for your attention; you read, and make note of some things you've learned. On Instagram you post photographs of your favorite pieces, and follow the curator on Twitter. Even though there are some postcards and coffee-table books that interest you in the gift shop, you avoid it because you'd have to look at materials portraying other kinds of art, and you find that unnecessary, baffling, and even a little upsetting. When you leave, you're proud of your commitment to this type of art, and the dedication you have to knowing everything about it. When your sister in law comments on Instagram that one of the paintings you've shared is "so bougie" you unfollow her. Later that week, when the curator you recently followed on Twitter posts a book review for a new book that denounces Impressionism as misunderstood by the masses and deeply pedestrian, you like several re-tweets that disagree with her, even though one calls her a "stupid bitch." You feel a little bad, but if she's the curator for those artworks at a major museum, she should be more careful what she shares that is untrue or harmful.

If we move from the way we personally encounter difference, to the seminal events many Americans see as related to the development of the interfaith movement, we see commonalities. I will accept that these historical instances—the first Parliament, *Nostra Aetate*, and 9/11—in American history are rich veins of gold that we are still mining, even if I am uncertain of their priority on my own list of "important historical events in interfaith." That is, many scholars and public voices are invested in the question, "When did interfaith begin in America?" Strangely, this question holds little interest for me. I sense that if interfaith has not been a part of every encounter between those who already lived in and those who immigrated to North America, difference was always present and either a galvanizing force for violence, or for positive movements of understanding, cooperation, learning, and change. However, even though I wouldn't frame a historical investigation of the emergence of interfaith dialogue and education as a question of genesis, I do acknowledge that these three cases in particular highlight something important. I see a common theme in each case, however—the opening of specific instances of disequilibrium for participants, and for those immediately after the events. These events were once shocking (in very different ways), and the shock and confusion were accessible to both scholars and those around any dinner table outside of Chicago. Our own realities are always incomplete. Events like these disrupt our previous knowledge of the world and then we are either welcomed—or forced—to confront the unknown. Eminent comparative theologian Catherine Cornille reminds us,

> Yet thought through to the end, it is the very realization of the ineffability of the ultimate reality that brings into perspective *the contingency of all finite expressions* of that reality, whereupon dialogue finds a basis that is both spiritual and theological.[46]

What is more shocking, more disconcerting, than the realization that life as we know it is being expanded? When this happens, other voices add their realities to our own, and we realize that what

---

46. Cornille, *The Im-Possibility of Interreligious Dialogue*, 213. Emphasis mine.

we thought we knew for sure was only provisional. And yet, as Cornille realizes, when we understand that perspective, we are getting closer to understanding something about ultimate reality—whether "ultimate reality" means the infinite nature of God or an afterlife, or whether it means something like "a more complete understanding of my relationships with other living beings in this world."[47] What is important about Cornille's reminder when I apply it to the development of inter-religious education is that she highlights the connection between realizations about complex questions and dialogue. I believe that one reason inter-religious education continues to grow is because inter-religious educators—as we have seen in the few I have surveyed here—make explicit these links between finite and provisional knowledge, encounters with difference that lead to fruitful realizations, and dialogue. Because inter-religious educators have been responsive to the needs of learners, the field has also been reflective and adapting as it grows.

As Clooney declares,

> If we do our work well, grounding scholarly commitments in faith, we will always be on the edge of failing in scholarship or failing in faith. Then we will be properly conflicted theologians, comparative theologians.[48]

"Properly conflicted"—yes, I think this is our vocation. To never rest, to seek disequilibrium, to invite more and more collaborators and lean into the unexpected. We could paraphrase Clooney and say, "If we do our work well, inter-religious educators will always be on the edges of disequilibrium, richly unsure of scholarship and blessedly unsure of faith. Then we will be properly learning." Clooney seems to sense that the very terms he charts are changing as second- and third-generation inter-religious theologians use them; he charts use of term "comparative theology" from 1700s onward, concluding,

> The older comparative theology seems, on the one hand, too comfortably immune to the complicated

---

47. Ibid.
48. Clooney, *Comparative Theology*, 30.

> implications of what is learned, and, on the other hand, too diffident about how a faith bravely vulnerable to scholarship might truly profit from the deep study of another tradition.[49]

I agree whole-heartedly that brave vulnerability is a necessary ingredient and that we benefit greatly when we do not know where we will end up.

Returning to Cornille, we are reminded that "If empathy entails more than a repetition or recognition of one's own past experiences, it thirdly requires a rich imagination,[50]" and "Empathy is explicitly dynamic.[51]" Empathetic, rich, imaginative, and dynamic: these are hallmarks of inter-religious educational spaces that foster disequilibrium, learning, collaboration, and change. Even as we seek to know more about what inter-religious learning looks like, and how to develop our expertise in it, we can begin—provisionally—with these motifs. As inter-religious educators, we will need to practice balancing what we know now, and the spaces beyond, for which we don't yet have language. In this practice, we will be conflicted, we might be impatient with the provisional nature of our work, and we may long for more stable forms of discourse. And yet: this practice, entered willingly, exposes us to the possible. Our webs of connection with one another are strengthened. Our ethical and religious practices are gilded with mystery/possibility as we return, ever-discursively, to reconsider what we thought we knew. Our ability to co-teach as members of shifting communities of meaning-makers will deepen our ability to learn, to enter dialogue, and to teach again.

All forms of education necessarily invoke and address disequilibrium as it precedes learning. Inter-religious education in particular deliberately sets out to invoke an encounter with something new—the very word "inter" as a prefix points to a plurality of viewpoints; perspectives will be raised amongst, between, or against others. Sometimes, the encounters are fraught with surprise, discomfort, or unexpected angst; at other times,

---

49. Ibid., 35.
50. Ibid., 153.
51. Ibid., 161.

the encounters provide an opportunity for deeper or renewed understanding of one or both perspectives. For these reasons, the process of inter-religious education demands that we be mindful about needs of those encountering alterity.

Previous research on resiliency has focused on children and young adults in therapeutic and school settings; some research has included belonging to a faith community as one factor in resiliency, but no one has connected resiliency as a trait that makes inter-religious learning more fruitful.

Time for Pause
The Breath that Will Sustain Us

If dialogue is essential to interfaith education, it would follow that those teaching interfaith in higher education settings would need to foster it explicitly. R., a Christian professor, shares how even initial experiences encountering religious difference can provide reflective impetus for positive stimulation towards integrative reconstruction. R. shared,

> That's why the dialogue thing is critically important in the community . . . Because it is beginning to say to people that, "You know it is actually safe that we are different. You are very disconcerted about this. But it is very safe that we're different. And so here, why don't you come up and we going to do it one month in the mosque, one month in the synagogue and one month in the church. If you are uncomfortable going anywhere else, come up when it is in synagogue. You know—you will sit in your own synagogue with a group of Muslims, a group of Christians, and three religious experts. You will watch that we can have two hours of civil conversation about topic that we can disagree on. Then we can all have kosher cookies and go home" . . . There was no explosion and we were not fighting and we did not have

to have police for security. Amazingly, people were quite shocked that happened in our northern suburbs.[1]

Many other interview participants gestured toward similar potentials for growth as aims for dialogue engagement.

French educator Jean Piaget, with his theory of constructivism (we learn by constructing meaning out of our experiences), reminds us that the assimilation of new knowledge first disrupts and then is integrated into one's understanding of the world. Inter-religious education in particular works best because inter-religious education is particularly invested in holding together difference—different ideas, different people, different categories, and different practices. That is, any new information or encounter provokes learning; because inter-religious education already deals with difference, inter-religious educators ought to be especially mindful of allowing for construction of new meaning with the material of alterity.

LeBaron so beautifully articulates how painful, and yet graceful, this "under construction" mode must be, writing: "When we encounter mystery (and conflict is often mysterious, tangled as it is in relational, personal, and cultural dynamics), we seek to understand it." For example: if Jesus is the Way, the Truth, and the Light, what of our neighbor who practices Dhighambra Jainism? One task of inter-religious education is to facilitate encounters and relationships in ways that allow participants to move past a craving for simplistic answers and to sit in a place of provisional, flexible, or imagined possibilities.

Or, to hear a similar exhortation from literature, as English novelist W. Somerset Maugham puts it, reminding us that all of our imagination begins with our earliest remembered interior spaces: "Men and women are not only themselves; they are also the region in which they were born, the city apartment or the farm in which they learned to walk, the games they played as children, the old wives' tale they overheard, the food they ate, the schools they attended, the poems they read, and the God they believed

---

1. R., in discussion with the author, October 2014.

in."[2] Who are you? Where were you born? Where did you learn to walk? What games did you play as a child? What stories did the old folks tell in your childhood? What food did you eat? What schools did you attend? What poems did you read? What God did you believe in?

And just as you are woven with all of these strands of memory, formation, and experience, so too are all who surround you. No one has had the exact experiences as you. When we meet and recognize, certain aspects of ourselves are heightened, or gilded, or offended, or broken. In relationship with others, we learn, hurt, suffer, create great beauty and art, feel more complete, understand loneliness, and approach what might be divine, what might be our best selves.

Berling elegantly describes this ballet of learning, relationship, and reflection with the following process; she writes:

> Unraveling, naming, and describing the threads of the learning process offer an interpretation of that process. The five threads are encountering difference or entering another world; one's initial response as a Christian; conversation and dialogue on several levels; living out what has been learned; and internalizing the process.[3]

I think the history of inter-religious educators could be described in a similar way: theologians and educators encountered difference, they sought respectful and fruitful ways to enter other worlds, they responded from their location as scholars, and they lived out what they learned in repositioning their work—all of this led to the development of inter-religious education. I am ending this section with Berling's voice because I think her scholarship, especially encapsulated in her *Guide for Interreligious Education*, parallels the development of the field as a whole. Her own curiosity and commitment to her students—as a teacher of comparative religions—led to the reflective and creative process that helped develop her leadership in inter-religious education.

---

2. Maugham, *The Razor's Edge*, 1–2.
3. Berling, *Understanding Other Religious Worlds*, 2.

The field itself has been responsive and inclusive; participants include students, theologians, mono-religious teachers, peace activists, and international communities of interfaith work. When Berling writes, "Learning in a diverse world requires not merely mastering some set of information but also learning to understand and negotiate areas of human difference, envisioning new ways of being and new possibilities,"[4] I also read, "*Inter-religious education* in a diverse world requires . . . learning to understand and negotiate areas of human difference and envisioning new possibilities." I believe that at this point in time, inter-religious education is well positioned to flourish, in large part because of its multiple strands of genealogy and its multiple ways of responding to the needs of teachers and learners. And we will flourish if we are willing to engage this entangling and renewing work.

What are capacities for inter-religious education, and how can we articulate and model them? The following capacities can be understood to be skills or dispositions that should be the fruit of successful interfaith engagement; note also the theologian or educator from which they emanate. They include: a willingness to be wrong and/or hear difficult truths (Boys and Lee), the ability to take others' perspectives, the ability to practice a posture of openness (Knitter), an empathetic imagination (Berling), conflict fluency (LeBaron and Pillay), a narrative imagination (Shaw, Rogers), and the ability to move these skills and dispositions into other contexts (Berling).

As students involved in interfaith engagement spend more time, relationship, and practice with these skills and dispositions, they will develop the leadership and facilitation skills to help other groups or members of their communities engage these practices. However, there is an artfulness to these practices; all of these theologians and educators note that they—even as experts—continue to practice these skills and dispositions. Later, we can more deeply explore these notions of "artfulness" and "practice."

A willingness to be wrong and/or hear difficult truths and the ability to practice a posture of openness: Developmental

---

4. Ibid., 26.

psychologists such as Piaget and Lev Vygotsky, as well as religious educators such as James Fowler, note that humans develop in stages—when one encounters something new, she has to work to incorporate it into her previous understanding of the world. This is also a practice—as students involved in interfaith engagement spend more time and practice with these skills, and show willingness to hear and engage, they will find those encounters less dangerous.

The ability to take others' perspectives: Perspective-taking practice can come about because of engagement with the arts (playwriting and performance, storytelling, mask-making) or through models of spiritual care and counseling (active listening, empathy and forgiveness practice). This skill is also related to critical thinking—the ability to hold within one's mind multiple viewpoints, including viewpoints that are very different, can help one read, learn, and think critically. Students studying law and debate, writers, and new physicians learning the art of diagnosing patients all benefit from perspective-taking practice. This practice is related to reflective practice.

An empathetic imagination and a narrative imagination: These are related to perspective-taking practice, and can also be fostered through the arts. In interfaith engagement, it is helpful for us to be able to imagine different horizons of time, family relationship, and emotions like shame and pride. It is necessary to be able to "read" the story of another with an openness of heart and a positive curiosity. When we are able to connect our small stories with greater narrative arcs, our engagement with others is enriched. Later, we will explore how narrative engagement can buttress and inform reflective practice, especially as a sustaining factor in resilience.

Alterity is a philosophical, anthropological term meaning "other" or "otherness." It can be seen to be an opposite for identity, or the opposite of one's self. In formal interfaith studies, we can talk about "negotiating alterity." Basically, this idea is, "When you encounter someone or something who is very different, how do you respond?"

Sometimes, if we are not feeling threatened, or if there are positive reasons for the encounter (a new family member, trying a new food, enjoying part of a vacation, being introduced by someone we trust like a minister or professor), we are comfortable.

Other times, we may feel an intense dislike, aversion, or fear. These negative responses may be heightened if we experience threats, including (even perceived) economic loss, loss of identity or importance, or during times of conflict and discord. One key objective of this book is to give you tools to "successfully" encounter and navigate alterity, and to lead others, too.

What is disequilibrium? If we are experiencing equilibrium, we are at a balanced state, we are composed, unruffled. However, all new experiences and information unbalance us, and this is a good thing. The following questions can help provoke some healthy disequilibrium:

- If I learn about other religions, will I lose part of my Christianity?
- What is a posture of openness?
- Are Allah and God really the same thing?
- Do we all pray to the same people?
- How do people who aren't religious participate in interfaith work?
- Do converts ever miss their old tradition?
- What is "holy envy"?

Which of these questions are most interesting to you? Which feel the most troubling, or provocative? Which would you like to be able to answer for your community?

When we are very little, we make mistakes all day long. We don't know all of the words for things, we fall frequently, our depth perception, agility, and precision with language are still not fully formed. Our balance is off. We lack the equilibrium that comes with age and experience.

Interfaith Grit: How Uncertainty Will Save Us

And when we are adults, we have that experience—but we resist disequilibrium. We like to think we have it all figured out, that our worlds are predictable and sensible, that our answers give solace. Sometimes they do. But when we encounter difference—and what is being alive in this world without encountering the new—we experience a kind of stress, a realization of disequilibrium.

And so, if we are committed to working with one another, and we understand that all real learning necessitates encountering new ideas, new people, new environments, new experiences—how do we withstand the stress that disequilibrium can bring?

Current research in inter-religious learning tells us that engaging with other traditions does more than widen our worldviews. Books like Paul Knitter's *Without Buddha I Could Not Be a Christian* have given many of us language to talk about what it means to become familiar with a new tradition or way of thinking, and how it influences the way we see our usual practices.

Learning is a process. A relationship is a process. Dialogue is a process. Before learning leads to transformation, we can take time to explore. We can compare our own tastes, habits, rituals, preferences, and prayers with others. Some will be similar. Some will surprise us. Some will be confusing, and others inspiring. As we learn to look, be aware of all of these impressions: fear, dislike, confusion, satisfaction, envy, surprise, disappointment, judgment, recognition, and inspiration. Initial connections and points of contrast may build a foundation for further analysis and even inspired practice. In this human endeavor, where we're better together, exploring with a posture of openness both affirms our shared humanity and helps keep us curious and ready to learn.

Who should be engaging this work? If you are curious about how to build your own resilience in the face of difference and uncertainty, these practices are for you. You will also find tools and practices in this book if the following situations resonate:

- Your workplace is religiously or culturally diverse, and you want to get along with your colleagues.

- You are a leader and need to understand difference and how to help your clients and employees thrive in spite of diversity.
- You work in public schools, hospitals, airports, municipalities, or with the general public as a first responder.
- You are a religious leader.
- You have family members from different denominations or faith traditions.
- You have left the tradition in which you were raised and now practice no religion, or a new religion.
- You travel frequently and want to be a good international visitor, businessperson, or tourist.
- You are afraid of immigrants in your country.
- You are angry at those who are afraid of immigrants in your country.
- You feel disenchanted with political and social processes that are supposed to build bridges and social infrastructure.
- You know a lot about different religions and cultures but less about how to lead inter-religiously.
- You don't know much about religion or culture, and want to learn *how* to learn.
- You lead book groups, and are looking for something both topical and transformative.
- You don't like other humans very much right now.
- You love other humans so much.

Shared interpretative activity generates social space. That is, looking together and asking questions together creates community. If you gather people around a concern or cause, you create a social space of common intentions and understandings. Sociologist William Schweiker calls such settings "spaces of reasons"; that is, settings in which people speak a common language and understand one another because they share a certain vocabulary and a certain set of perceptions. Practical theologian Lewis S. Mudge builds upon this concept of shared reasoning spaces to argue for inter-religious dialogue in *The Gift of Responsibility: The Promise of Dialogue Among Christians, Jews, and Muslims*. He writes, "But in a reflexive, multicultural world, the symbols by which we interpret the meaning of our acting will lack coherence unless the living religious traditions find ways of entering into one another's reasoning spaces."[5] How can we prepare ourselves to enter these strange new spaces? Reflective practice is essential.

What is "reflective practice"? Reflective practice encompasses the following possibilities:

- Receiving direct instruction or modeling in stepping back, reflecting, and connecting one's experiences with one's interior life.
- Time outside of explicit, direct instruction. This might be used to pause and reflect upon what has been learned and can include questioning, daydreaming, building relationships between ideas, and experiencing joy and frustration. Then, the learner can return to the instructional setting primed to continue encountering new ideas.

In short, reflective practice is a necessary ingredient for successful interfaith engagement, and also has healing properties for those of us buffeted by exposure to countless ideas, conflicts, and fears in our global, daily lives. Reflective practice makes us more resilient. And even though these two practices can be taught, modeled, and practiced separately, competencies in one can lead to stronger competencies in the other, and practicing them together grows both competencies in a way that means the overall capacity to practice reflection and remain in learning spaces with tenacity is greater than one's capacities in either.

Clooney's work in comparative theology allowed for the new field of interfaith work to take root and flourish. The idea of "practice" is instrumental in understanding how interfaith education

---

5. Mudge, The Gift of Responsibility, 129.

works. Clooney describes the practice of doing comparative theology in his text of the same name; he writes, "like all forms of theology, comparative theology is a form of study."[6] Clooney defines interreligious dialogue as "point[ing] to actual conversations." Actual conversations. It is not enough for us to watch television programs about other cultures, or follow religious leaders on Twitter, or practice Buddhism in a yoga studio, or read about Islam in books. The "religion and spirituality" section of a bookstore may be appealing, and may in fact have much to offer us in terms of mere knowledge, but dialogue requires conversation with other people. Relationship. Risk.

Clooney suggests that engaging in a posture of learning leads to new intellectual insights. Similarly, in interfaith dialogue, we learn from one another—but this kind of learning influences both our scholarship and our personal religious commitments. We have here two poles: first, the concept that openness to learning rekindles and even creates new scholarship. This is an intellectual benefit to learning. Second, we have the concept that learning from one another—not from theological study, from text study, or from comparative religious work—can change us. Learning new information is one part. And then we must turn and share (or test in real life) what we've learned. That is, we learn and then we turn to share our new insights; this pattern is part of reflective practice.

Before we begin exploring how reflective practice helps us become more resilient, it is important to be clear about what we mean by "risk" and "vulnerability" in interfaith settings. Interfaith settings include the workplace, parenting communities, online, restaurants and shops, airports; anywhere we encounter people who are different can be an interfaith setting. Sometimes, the risk feels positive, like when we try a new kind of food. Sometimes, the risk feels negative, like when airport security asks us to step out of line for additional questioning because we aren't dressed like others in that context.

When I began my research for this project, I interviewed ten interfaith educators at colleges, seminaries, and universities across

6. Clooney, *Comparative Theology*, 4.

the United States. I asked them about their experiences teaching in their classes, and in the community. One theme that emerged early, was echoed throughout the initial interviews, and was confirmed in second interviews, was the notion that "dissonance" is nearly always a factor in education, and in interfaith education specifically. In music, dissonance is a lack of harmony. In politics and culture, dissonance is a clash or tension between beliefs. In education and psychology, dissonance is the shaky feeling we experience when we have one worldview, but come across new information or experiences that make us doubt our prior knowledge or deeply held beliefs.

I asked my interfaith colleagues, "When students are able to do really well in interfaith settings, what habits, attitudes, knowledge or practice do you see in them that make that possible?"

Their answers create a provisional portrait of dissonance in interfaith learning settings that is helpful for our understanding of this challenge. Interview participant answers include the following remarks:

> The students do get frustrated, because they hear not dual narratives but multiple narratives. There are not two narratives. There are fifty narratives. The students do find this a little frustrating.

> You sort of have to dialogue before dialogue. You are in inter-religious dialogues, but you don't know what the word "religion" means. Learning the words we presume mean the same things, don't mean the same thing is a huge part of this and people who are part of this have that kind of linguistic flexibility—that complicated business of overlapping semantic fields that don't perfectly correspond [with] each other.

> Everybody is insecure about their identity. So drawing borders is an important activity; it tells me who is in and who is out. At this moment with globalization and increasing pluralism in our increased society and context, the ability to draw those borders reassures me—that kind of reassures me I know who I am, because I can draw

the borders. It is very disconcerting to discover that the borders are strange.

The Palestinian boys who are one moment throwing rocks at the wall and when they get bored ten minutes later, they play soccer. We understand playing soccer but we don't understand throwing rocks at the wall.

That disjunction between "different" and "like" is, I think, very important to see but it is very unsettling to see, all those [kids] just throwing rocks at the wall. "I want all those women frumpy wearing burqas like I saw in the Taliban. I want all of those people angry all the time rather than frumpy. I don't want to see young men and women not dressed like rabbis."

I think there's some tension—so for instance, if I'm in the room with a bunch of other, let's say, Muslim academics or theologians, it's a lot more difficult than, from—maybe because people understand experiences very differently and maybe something that I learned is not the same that some, that somebody else there [learned.]

Sometimes people are afraid to speak up because they're afraid to look bad in front of their co-religionists, or look ignorant in front of their co-religionists. Or be, you know . . . being embarrassed is a huge risk.

We all have things at stake and we all have histories we are a part of and the degree to which we take responsibility for those is really varied . . . what is my responsibility for a position that I might not personally hold but that my traditions have been responsible for perpetuating, causing a lot of harm in the name of—those are some of the harder questions that we try to get students to really wrestle with a little.

Here we see examples of learners' frustration, fear, tension, disjunction, feeling disconcerted, insecurity, presumption, and a complicated relationship with terms and norms once taken for granted. Have we not all felt many of these things when we listen to the news or engage in social media, on a daily basis? These are the emotions that arise in interfaith encounters that necessitate some care and thoughtfulness on our part around teaching and fostering capacities that enable one another to grow through these feelings and learn. How often do you wrestle with "harder questions" about race, economics, culture, religion, and how to participate in civil discourse? When are you tempted to draw borders so you know who is like you, and who is not? When are those borders healthy and helpful, and when do they keep you from being fully human?

Specifically, if we are resilient, we may be able to find and use resources to succeed in diverse settings no matter what. If we find time to reflect, debrief, decompress, rest, and reengage on our own, we will be able to successfully integrate the new information. Indeed, when survey participants were given the option to make additional comments at the conclusion of the survey, one participant admitted, "If I want to present the new material with the subtlety and depth that leads to serious reflection, I probably don't have time for that to actually happen in the course structure. But I do expect it to be built into their lives."

Reflective practice is so necessary that we cannot endeavor to build interfaith engagement unless we commit time and resources to it; reflective practice builds capacities for resilience in a way that allows us to better encounter difference and dissonance, and then better learn and lead.

Reflection is an intrinsic part of self-understanding. Many religions teach spiritual reflection practices that are related to general aspects of reflective practice. Some examples include meditation, praying the Rosary, walking a labyrinth, making silent pilgrimage, Ignatian spiritual practice, and journaling. And in recent decades, reflective practice has become important in business and leadership in the secular world.

Donald Schön's *The Reflective Practitioner* facilitated the development of reflective practice as an ongoing skill that could be strengthened into something akin to virtuosity for professionals (such as architects or psychiatrists). For Schön, the ideas of "puzzling" and "reflection-in-action" are key. He provides examples and reflects upon them, developing his theory that with practice, professionals can create new schema when encountering disruptions in their daily work, and grow the variety and type of responses they have for confronting challenges. Many of us dislike feeling puzzled. When we approach a subway map or restaurant menu, we don't want to work too hard to figure it out. We're easily annoyed. Or when someone joins our team at work, and they don't participate in meetings or monthly birthday celebrations in a typical way, we are puzzled, but it isn't positive. Or when we attend a community meeting and someone refuses to shake our hand, we are puzzled and may immediately dislike or distrust the person. We work to make our lives flow smoothly, and smoothly often means "with as few disruptions or puzzles as possible."

Schön is interested in our ability to respond to changing challenges with creativity; he noticed that when we reflect upon the way we respond, we get better at solving problems. As Schön puts it, "In the most generic sense, to experiment is to act in order to see what the action leads to. The most fundamental experimental question is, 'What if?'"[7]

The process of asking oneself "What if?" becomes a galvanizing, life-affirming practice that allows one to connect prior experience and knowledge to the current context, and to resist foreclosing judgment and wait for additional insight.

When we foreclose judgment, we quickly categorize any new experience or information into a pre-existing category in our mind—and then we move on. This food is unclean, this person is rude, this commentator is biased, this driver isn't professional, these students aren't safe, those police officers are cowards . . . As information and experiences wash over us, and especially when we are confronted with challenging or painful information, our adult ("experienced") brains quickly label and categorize, and we remain comfortable, but unchanged.

Initially, Schön was struck by the fact that many experienced and intelligent professionals were gifted with knowledge about their jobs, but seemed unable to deal with the disruptions of working life. He noticed, "As the tasks change, so will the demands for

---

7. Schön, *The Reflective Practitioner*, 145.

usable knowledge, and the patterns of task and knowledge are inherently unstable."[8] What areas in your life could be described as "inherently unstable"? What features of your community, or political party, or nation, feel unstable?

This notion of dealing with situations that are "inherently unstable" provide rich insight when we come to understanding key competencies for interfaith dialogue because fruitful learning frequently comes from encounters that hold multiplicities of possible views or outcomes. Schön called these unstable situations "messes."[9] This metaphor is one we hear echoed in popular discourse: "She's a hot mess." "That bill was a mess when it got to the House." "The hearings were a mess." "The summit was a failure, a complete mess." And even, in tongue-in-cheek self-recognition, "Bless this mess." Being human is a messy endeavor!

Schön noticed that professionals were often challenged by "the multiplicity of conflicting views"[10] when they sought answers to their dilemmas. And yet, more multiplicities often mean we are working in richer or more challenging contexts. Few of us wish for more boring work lives; how do we balance our intellectual development and expertise with places of "messiness" that we encounter and might resist? Schön connected this challenge with the work of self-awareness, which leads to reflective practice; he writes,

> In sum, when leading professionals write or speak about their own crisis of confidence, they tend to focus on the mismatch of traditional patterns of practice and knowledge to features of the practice situation—complexity, uncertainty, instability, uniqueness, and value conflict—of whose importance they are increasingly aware. Surely this is a laudable exercise in self-criticism.[11]

Complexity, uncertainty, instability, uniqueness, and value conflict—not only are these prevalent in professional contexts, they are the very stuff of education and human relationship. Teachers

8. Ibid., 15.
9. Ibid.
10. Ibid., 17.
11. Ibid., 18.

attempt to gently create complexity so that students might build creative strategies for addressing uncertainty in all places and forms. As Schön puts it, students (of all sorts) must live in a space that "[has] to do with the relationship between changing things and understanding them."[12]

A space between wanting or needing to change things, and understanding them; this is a place of pause, a place of not knowing. One role of educators and religious leaders is to make that space habitable. We need to be able to live there, and hopefully thrive there. For example, J. is a Christian professor of interfaith studies, teaching in a seminary and with an ongoing relationship with a nearby rabbinical school. When she reflects on how to foster positive interfaith capacities in her classes, she describes wanting to make those spaces not only habitable, but inviting for the kind of work she deems necessary. J. shares,

> Creating a space in the classroom where people were invited to be a little vulnerable, appropriately vulnerable—to share a full spectrum of who they are required modeling integration, modeling a little vulnerability, modeling a little playfulness, modeling risk taking. At the same time, creating a space for risk-taking also required dependability, hard work, attention to detail and responsiveness on my part as the professor.[13]

This kind of space would be amenable to risk-taking, reflection, and vulnerability. Reflective practice can be a means to uncover possibly fruitful ways to live with "changing things."

By 2005, when Germaine L. Taggart and Alfred P. Wilson write *Promoting Reflective Thinking in Teachers: 50 Action Strategies*, reflective practice was considered so essential that teacher educators developed ways to foster and assess reflective practice in novice teachers. *Promoting Reflective Thinking* includes a "plan of action for continued growth in reflective thinking," with particular attention to the space between understanding things and changing them, or, as Taggart and Wilson notice,

12. Ibid., 147.
13. J., in discussion with the author, October 2014.

> A strategic plan of action will allow practitioners to use what has been learned about reflection to create a long-range plan that incorporates existing and newly acquired schemata and continual feedback. Through such a plan, the natural tendency of adults to problem solve and to resolve discrepancies between what is and what should be addressed can be enhanced.[14]

Taggart and Wilson's text is an excellent example of how far reflective practice has come in twenty-two years because it has all of the representative hallmarks of a rich and contemporary text for teachers and teacher trainers; it's full of worksheets, practice lesson plans, places for on-the-spot reflection, small case studies, recommendations, and suggestions from master teachers. It's divided up into fifty action plans that are welcoming, doable, and avoid overwhelming the reader or teacher with too much at once. Like any good practice, reflective practice via Taggart and Wilson is about jumping in and starting.

We also see a direct link between the kinds of thinking Schön encouraged and the activities that have made their way into the reflective teacher's repertoire. Taggart and Wilson write,

> Strategies used to promote reflective thinking . . . include observational learning; reflective journals; practicum activities, such as reflective teaching and microteaching; mental-model strategies, such as metaphors and repertory grids; narrative strategies, such as story, autobiographical sketches, and case study; establishing technology-enhanced learning communities; and action research.[15]

Similarly, just as the meta-cognitive ability to make choices in new situations is essential to Schön's project, Taggart and Wilson's activities are intended to foster "the ability to make defensible choices and view an event with open-mindedness is also indicative of reflecting at a dialectical level."[16] Metacognition is the ability to

---

14. Taggart and Wilson, *Promoting Reflective Thinking in Teachers*, xii.
15. Ibid., xii–xiii.
16. Ibid., 5.

think about our thinking. Practicing metacognition allows us to consider, before we react. It can be as simple as reading a headline or Facebook post, feeling adrenaline or a self-righteous pleasure surge, and then pausing to ask, "Why am I feeling this way?" (Remember: "How am I feeling?" and "What do I need?") Over time, our abilities to think about our thinking help us to become more mature in our judgment and actions, and build complex relationships with ideas and people who we disagree with. Taggart and Wilson's recommendations and strategies are common traits in teacher education literature that supports reflective practice in teachers. Does your workplace or chosen career depend on reflective practice? Do you have time in your workday to think about what you're doing and what you're thinking? Or is work too rapid and messy? Lives without time for pause can make us feel that there is no time for exploration or reconsidering: we must stick to the facts, and deal with things as straightforwardly as possible.

Schön often uses figurative language in his attempts to describe the artfulness with which we demonstrate the capacity of reflective practice. Taggart and Wilson also emphasize the importance of metaphorical thinking; from their elucidation of the power of metaphor, we can move directly into the field of religious education, where the power of story is honored and sought after. Schön describes the tricky nature of putting one's finger on exactly how to frame a new puzzle into existing schemas of experience; he writes,

> When we go about the spontaneous, intuitive performance of the actions of everyday life, we show ourselves to be knowledgeable in a special way. Often we cannot say what it is that we know. When we try to describe it we find ourselves at a loss, or we produce descriptions that are obviously inappropriate. Our knowing is ordinarily tacit, implicit in our patterns of action and in our feel for the stuff with which we are dealing. It seems right to say that our knowing is *in* our action.[17]

---

17. Schön, *The Reflective Practitioner*, 49. Emphasis original.

"Often we cannot say what it is we know." Indeed, one challenge of dealing with intellectual, emotional, or spiritual disequilibrium is even beginning to name what it is we're facing. One benefit of highlighting the cognitive process of "knowing-in-action" and recognizing it as part of a practice is that it takes the pressure off finding immediate answers or even finding one answer at all. Instead, our focus on opening a space of provisional knowing-in-action favors process over immediate action.

Metaphors are one tool for dealing with "descriptions that are obviously inappropriate." Metaphors may allow us to practice thinking about a new concept or situation before we are ready to embrace it fully. Taggart and Wilson focus on working with metaphors in reflective practice because they recognize that teachers who can learn to reach for metaphoric thinking will grow in reflective practice. In addition, thinking in metaphors is a process that can be modeled and shared with others, which creates the opportunity for communal meaning-making and reflective circles of practice, both of which support pre-service teachers and reflective practitioners in any profession. Taggart and Wilson identify several key aspects of metaphors as tools for reflective practice, writing:

> Metaphors can: aid in self-exploration of beliefs and values, help form boundaries and conditions for members, assist in simplifying and clarifying problems, help to summarize thoughts, enable and limit meaning, help develop alternative ways of looking at a topic (problem reframing), serve as bridges between a schema and new constructs, help form judgments about educational issues, assist with communication of abstract ideas, demonstrate underlying connections, [and] gain insights into what is not yet understood.[18]

We can imagine that if one were creating a reflective practice workshop, and facilitating techniques to aid reflection upon what is currently unknown and what is already known, the use of

---

18. Taggart and Wilson. *Promoting Reflective Thinking in Teachers*, 169.

metaphors as described by Taggart and Wilson could serve as tasks to welcome novice reflective practitioners.

In his description of why current students, residents of his city, and even US Christians currently experience visible signs of dissonance and anxiety, R. noted that two poems[19] from the Victorian period perfectly capture some of what Christians are experiencing in his religiously diverse, multicultural, multiracial, Southern US city. When elaborating on the idea that Christians in his city are finally realizing their city might not be Christian, he shares,

> There is this massive Victorian anxiety about the loss [of] faith and that in Yeats's "The Second Coming." These poems resonate today because many of the same things are in our culture and in our midst. That anxiety level is high here in [my city]. We are in the last redoubt of Christendom here. We have huge mega-churches and pastors are still important public figures here. They have the ear of the city council and they are on the news. But the anxiety is still here. When who we really are gets exposed . . . we're very slow to let go of that but we are not the same city. That's why the dialogue thing is critically important in the community.[20]

R.'s discursive movement to including literary expressions of social dissonance related to religious difference is both a fluent demonstration of metaphor and an example of the way depicting dissonance in inter-religious classrooms can be helped by using figurative language or imaginative examples. Indeed, the very thrust of "The Sea of Faith" deals with the speaker's recognition of the "eternal note of sadness" brought by understanding that faith is no more. In the latter half of the poem, Arnold writes:

---

19. I have a background in Victorian literature and I connected anxiety about perceived social changes in the Victorian period to R.'s descriptions of what he sees in his students. In agreement, the two poems he offered as illustrative are Matthew Arnold's "Dover Beach" and William Butler Yeats's "The Second Coming."

20. R., in discussion with the author, October 2014.

> The Sea of Faith[21]
> Was once, too, at the full, and round earth's shore
> Lay like the folds of a bright girdle furled.
> But now I only hear
> Its melancholy, long, withdrawing roar,
> Retreating, to the breath
> Of the night-wind, down the vast edges drear
> And naked shingles of the world.
>
> Ah, love, let us be true
> To one another! for the world, which seems
> To lie before us like a land of dreams,
> So various, so beautiful, so new,
> Hath really neither joy, nor love, nor light,
> Nor certitude, nor peace, nor help for pain;
> And we are here as on a darkling plain
> Swept with confused alarms of struggle and flight,
> Where ignorant armies clash by night.

The work of the research participants in this study indicates that even without "certitude," there might well still be peace.

As it turns out, part of reflective practice that has been picked up by all those after Schön, from middle school coaches to Chinese language school directors, is the ability to turn one's mind to the problem with creativity. Schön calls it "naming and framing"; he writes,

> When we set the problem, we select what we will treat as the "things" of the situation, we set the boundaries of our attention to it, and we impose upon it a coherence which allows us to say what is wrong and in what directions the situation needs to be changed. Problem setting is a process in which, interactively, we *name* the things to

---

21. R. misremembered the title of "Dover Beach," calling it "The Sea of Faith" in his interview; this accidental retitling reveals his understanding of what the poem is about and why it might apply to the dissonance experienced by his students and program participants.

which we will attend and *frame* the context in which we will attend to them.²²

We note that "problem setting" is an inherently interactive process, according to Schön. This quality may be why so many professionals in the caring professors have adopted and adapted Schön's initial premises. These include those working in teaching, caring for the very young and very old, coaching, facilitating, and in conflict resolution and mediation. By the 1990s, teacher education programs had successfully incorporated the notion of "reflective practitioner" to describe masterful teachers who used reflective practice artfully and consistently. The concept of "reflective practice," has included, over the years, ideas including "reflective thinking," "critically reflective practice," "critical thinking," and "critical reflection."

In both setting a problem and in holding an idea apart to allow the light of reflection to shine upon it, casting lantern shadows of new understanding, the use of metaphor or copulas is necessary and allows for a flexibility of mind that, with practice, enables the thinker to encounter increasingly different contexts with curiosity, not paralysis. In *Principles of Instrumental Logic*, John Dewey uses the linguistic term copula²³ to help readers imagine this process. Dewey was a philosopher, logician, and educator; Schön was writing not for educators but for professionals looking to become more open, flexible, and virtuosic in their processes. So, while the latter spoke of metaphors as a way to help us describe the way we think about puzzles, Dewey is attempting to elucidate the very thought processes as we think about them. For this reason, Dewey's writing also creates a kind of primer on reflective thought that we will find useful not only as we consider

---

22. Schön, *The Reflective Practitioner*, 40. Emphasis original.

23. Copula is the linguistic term for linking verb, and can be seen in the sentence "The bridge is over the river;" a copula links the subject from the predicate. In Dewey's use, a copula is itself a bridge, linking a known concept to an unknown one for long enough for us to become comfortable with it—to incorporate it into our experience. See Dewey, *Principles of Instrumental Logic*, 36.

reflective practice à la Schön, but also as we reimagine it as an essential ingredient in inter-religious education.

Dewey begins his discussion of the use of the copula in perception, and in encountering the new, by writing,

> On the side of the subject [of judging something new in reality] the same difficulty appears. The whale is real. It meets us in perception. But when we examine the subject it is at the mercy of the same judgment. There was a time when "whale" was only "this." By a long series of investigations and judgments it has become real. By condensation of knowledge the whale is taken as given but is a concept, a former judgment, "This is a whale." The subject is always a union of previous predicates, abstractions. Then the function of the copula being to assert reality, both subject and predicate appear to be abstractions. One abstraction is asserted of the other.[24]

We can imagine a teacher early in her practice, having firmly in mind how she intends to address students who refuse to look her in the eye when she is disciplining them. Then, she learns that different cultures have different ways of understanding looking in the eyes of those in authority. Her thought process might unfold in the following way: "This [looking at me in the eye] is respect. Looking at my feet while I am speaking is disrespect." But (to quote Dewey) "'By a long series of investigations,' I know now that looking at my feet is also respect."

At an early point, "respect shown by looking at feet" was an unknown, and then an abstraction. By use of copula, the abstraction became visible as part of (a new) reality. Then, with practice (now leaving the realm of imagination into actual trial and error in reality), the teacher is able to recognize respect shown in more than one way. If you read about the same international incident on both Breitbart.com and Salon.com, do you see two truths, or truth shown (even inadvertently) in more than one way?

Dewey notes, "The significance of judgment is in the *process* of judgment, not in its completion. When judgment is completed

24. Ibid., 36.

there is no judgment, but a certain value."[25] That is, when we are judging (figuring out how to categorize something new, and how to incorporate it into our practice), it is that very work that is valuable, and that leads to our growth as practitioners. We should not despair that we will not know how to handle every challenge, or bemoan the sheer volume of new ideas or puzzles we encounter, but instead focus on growing in our metaphorical abilities so we can meet difference with openness, quickness of comparison, and alacrity in entering the process. In the next section, an investigation into narrative pedagogies will build upon our understanding of the importance of metaphorical thinking. As we shall see, in religious and inter-religious education students and participants frequently encounter "new truth" and static, unfolding aspects of (an ever-incomplete) reality. Copulas and metaphors give us moving frames upon which to hang new material as we make sense of it.

Schön's *The Reflective Practitioner* explores how professionals can think about their thinking so that their problem-solving might be most artful and benefit from ongoing reflection. For Schön, professionals include but are not limited to managers, architects, and therapists. Their problems are the stuff of everyday work: how to design a school where classrooms are both functional and inspirational, or how to help a young resident psychiatrist support his patient. Schön notes that professionals must be able to balance their goals with various unknowns that arise moment by moment. Dealing with uncertainty and being able to "puzzle" through work situations enable professionals to do their jobs well.

Schön introduces his definition of "puzzling" as he describes the artfulness with which professionals must engage in their work; he writes,

> Usually reflection on knowing-in-action goes together with reflection on the stuff at hand. There is some puzzling, or troubling, or interesting phenomenon with which the individual is trying to deal. As he tries to make sense of it, he also reflects on the understandings

25. Ibid., 44. Emphasis mine.

which have been implicit in his action, understandings which he surfaces, restructures, and embodies in further action. It is this entire process of reflection-in-action which is central to the "art" by which practitioners sometimes deal well with situations of uncertainty, instability, uniqueness, and value conflict.[26]

Here he also introduces the verb "knowing-in-action," which includes both the concept and points to a kind of reflection that later scholars pick up and include in various curricula and training materials. We note that Schön identifies a sequence of responses from the individual as they are presented with the "stuff at hand." First, they are troubled—the new information or encounter disrupts current practice. Next, in attempting to understand, they reflect on their current action, previous actions, and what they might do next. *They draw upon prior experience and knowledge to create a schema that will allow them to deal with the new.*

Schön draws upon both John Dewey and Jean Piaget to construct the reflection process. Piaget's theory of disequilibrium is echoed in the "troubling . . . phenomenon" that leads to a shift in thinking and action. In Dewey's *Logic: Theory of Inquiry*, he identifies situations that are "logically indeterminate"[27] and describes the anxiety they create. We are forced to reflect upon them and work to make meaning. Schön takes Dewey's and Piaget's focus on how the learner responds to the unknown a step further, positing that when we consider how we are responding to the problem, we are participating in solving it. It is the process of reflection itself that leads to successful practice. Schön writes,

> When we set the problem, we select what we will treat as the "things" of the situation, we set the boundaries of our attention to it, and we impose upon it a coherence which allows us to say what is wrong and in what directions the situation needs to be changed. Problem setting is a process in which, interactively, we *name* the things to

---

26. Schön, *The Reflective Practitioner*, 50.
27. Dewey, *The Theory of Inquiry*, 135.

which we will attend and *frame* the context in which we will attend to them.[28]

In other words, active reflection upon the problem—just after one notices the disruption—includes naming and (re-)framing it to create a container that will allow one to puzzle through it successfully.

According to Schön, professionals grow in their ability to do this; Schön likens the skill of entering zones of puzzling to the work of an artist. Indeed, he declares, "It is this entire process of reflection-in-action which is central to the 'art' by which practitioners sometimes deal well with situations of uncertainty, instability, uniqueness, and value conflict."[29] While "often we cannot say what it is that we know,"[30] participation in the "process of disruption," unknowing, knowing that one doesn't know, and then artful comparison to past experiences in search of similarities, into invention of a new response—this is reflection-in-action. What would your community look like if you emphasized pondering and process over leadership and knowledge-transmission? If you practiced pausing instead of "education"? If initiatives to suspend judgment were as popular as consciousness-raising endeavors? We know that time for pause greatly increases our mental health, emotional skills, and abilities to live and lead in the world—so why don't we invest time, resources, and programming into reflective practice?

Currently, reflective practice has been used as a primary source for education and professional development in three disparate fields: teacher training, nursing, and writing center facilitators working in higher education. Inter-religious educators can learn from all three of these groups; each uses key concepts of reflective practice, as well as adding content and methods unique to each audience. For example, writing center instructors and coaches hope to foster "metacognition" about the writing process in their students. Students who do not understand themselves to be good writers often do not use methods of self-talk, mental practice, or

---

28. Schön, *The Reflective Practitioner*, 40. Emphasis original.
29. Ibid., 50.
30. Ibid., 49.

reflection about their writing processes. Writing center coaches include direct instruction and modeling about reflection-in-action both in their work with students and in their own professional development programs.

Reflection-in-action is used by teachers in both reflective practice and action research; both fields and ways of teaching utilize Schön's original context to help pre-service and novice teachers develop the ongoing, continuous practice of reflection-in-action in their teaching and in their personal professional development. Interestingly, Schön never uses an educator for one of his examples; he is grounded in his own context, thinking about how organizations develop and are managed. However, his fingerprints are all over later work by and for educators.

By 2005, former teachers and teacher educators Germaine L. Taggart and Alfred P. Wilson had created a handbook for teachers and teacher trainers that exemplifies the absorption of Schön's philosophy into education. In their *Promoting Reflective Thinking in Teaches: 50 Action Strategies*, Taggart and Wilson name dozens of attributes that identify a teacher as a "reflective practitioner." They write,

> Reflective practitioners: identify and analyze problems and situations, look at problems relative to educational, social, and ethical issues, critically consider contextual and pedagogical factors, use a rational problem-solving approach, make intuitive, creative interpretations and judgments, are metacognitively, analytically, and instructionally skillful, possess self-efficacy, intrinsic motivation, and a desire for lifelong learning, are open to experimentation and new innovations, experience job satisfaction, make decisions consciously and carefully, view situations from multiple perspectives, set personal short-term and long-term goals, plan and monitor actions, then evaluate results of those actions, have essential skills for attaining and using information, correct understandings of

underlying facts, procedures, and skills, consider general characteristics of so-called best practice, are flexible in a search for alternative explanations, use evidence in supporting or evaluating a decision or position, have a commitment to values (e.g., all students can learn), have a strong commitment to systematic and rational reflective thinking, show responsiveness to educational needs of students, question personal aims and actions, constantly review instructional goals, methods, and materials, are a proactive force in education, are intellectually perceptive to multiple and novel ideas, are committed to problem resolution (wholeheartedness), commit adequate resources to reflective thinking (time as well as physical, mental, and emotional energy), welcome peer review, critique, and advice, write (journal) events reflectively.[31]

Here we have enough competencies and capacities to create an entire curriculum and assessment model for interfaith activists. We notice that aspects from Schön, such as encountering the disruption with a positive attitude, seeking to connect prior experiences and ideas, willingness to try new ideas, and participating in ongoing reflection, are embedded throughout Taggart's and Wilson's identifying features. In addition, Taggart and Wilson deliberately include time, space, and resources for one to reflect. They are, in a way, seeking to systematize (and even, given their packaging of the book for teacher education programs, institutionalize) reflective practice for teachers.

Reflective practice can be taught in a multitude of ways. Specifically, Taggart and Wilson recommend *journaling, storytelling, study circles,* and *"microteaching"*[32] as practices that foster reflection. It is important to note that Taggart and Wilson (like many of their peers) seek to *assess* reflective thinking, which is also an extension of Schön's original intentions. They write, "The benefits of reflective thinking are great. But how do you know where an individual functions as a reflective practitioner? How can you establish a baseline so that growth in reflection can be assessed?

31. Taggart and Wilson, *Promoting Reflective Thinking in Teachers*, 38.
32. Ibid., xii–xiii.

What constitutes evidence of reflection?"[33] These very questions indicate the importance of reflective practice in teacher preparation programs—the attention to assessment (and replicability) points to the value of reflective practice in teaching communities.

While Taggart and Wilson have designed their reflective practice for fostering ideas for teachers, they clearly can be adapted for teachers to use with students. In later chapters where we discuss applications of the findings of this research, we will explore possible adaptations more fully. Journaling is used widely in classrooms for a variety of reasons. For reflective practice specifically, they allow teachers to interact directly with students and students' thinking about their thinking. Storytelling develops a student's ability to both frame and re-frame their own experiences, as well as develop a posture of listening which can lead to perspective taking practice. Both of these skills are aspects of reflective practice. And finally, study circles allow for consistent relationship-building, which can create a safe container for encountering new or disruptive ideas and reflecting upon them. Within study circles, students can also try out solutions to common puzzles, and make use of multiple points of view. Even microteaching can be practiced by students and participants in interfaith engagement.

Taggart and Wilson describe mini lessons, in which novice teachers first practice using a new method or technique with peers. This allows them to try out new ideas, and to make themselves vulnerable among peers before taking the plunge with students. We can also imagine university students in an inter-religious context, for example, using the model of "mini lessons" to practice facilitating dialogue among stakeholders in their own communities, to practice giving a sermon or speech that draws upon comparative theologies, or working to solve a case study. Microteaching includes a debriefing component where peers can ask questions and the facilitator can reflect upon their own experience in the moment, with peers who help them understand and process the experience.

---

33. Ibid., 33.

In *Curriculum Action Research: A Handbook of Methods and Resources for the Reflective Practitioner*, James McKernan extends the concept of reflective practice and applies it to a form of research. That is, he posits, "the unifying theme is that all action research is a form of *reflective inquiry* governed by rigorous principles, or canons of procedure."[34] Like Schön, McKernan also likens the practice of reflective action to "the skills of the graffiti artist, dancer and composer,"[35] that are developed through inquiry and experience. For McKernan, the entire point of inquiry is understanding, which can lead to action towards improvement.[36] Teachers are in a unique position because their daily practice—fraught with minor disequilibriums and disruptions, even positive—is ripe for reflection-in-action.

The concept of "reflective practice," has included, over the years, ideas including "reflective thinking," "critically reflective practice," "critical thinking," and "critical reflection." If this capacity can be taught and practiced by professionals, why can it not be taught and practiced by students?

Is reflective practice essential for inter-religious learning? Despite the fact that (to our knowledge) Schön did not consider inter-religious education when he wrote his seminal *The Reflective Practitioner*, many of his concepts and descriptions of ways of knowing seem well suited for inter-religious education. In this section, we will connect Schön's concepts with ideas from narrative pedagogy in consideration of best practices in inter-religious education.

Inter-religious education can involve explicit instruction, or may come out of organic student encounters within a class. In either case, participants must work to identify and articulate their own interior spaces even as they share them with others, experience disruptions to their understanding of the world, and encounter accounts of the interior spaces of others. Sometimes,

---

34. *Curriculum Action Research*, 31. Emphasis original.

35. Ibid., 49.

36. This notion of "improvement," with an embedded idea of "growth," connects with our notion that inter-religious education must aim for change, transformation, or growth for individuals and communities.

our self-knowledge doesn't manifest until it comes into contact with the alterity of others. This contact is an example of what Schön considered a unique, puzzling situation that calls for a new response. Schön articulates this idea of as-yet unmanifested self-knowledge. He writes:

> When we go about the spontaneous, intuitive performance of the actions of everyday life, we show ourselves to be knowledgeable in a special way. Often we cannot say what it is that we know. When we try to describe it we find ourselves at a loss, or we produce descriptions that are obviously inappropriate. Our knowing is ordinarily tacit, implicit in our patterns of action and in our feel for the stuff with which we are dealing. It seems right to say that our knowing is *in* our action.[37]

So, inter-religious encounters might be understood as pregnant places where, at a loss to describe our response, we must move nimbly and gracefully within the moment—knowing and acting at the same time. For example, if someone is in the midst of conversation with another, and his thoughts about the afterlife are in question, he must—all at once—measure his response, consider what his tradition tells him, intuit what his classmate might know or fear, and identify how comfortable he feels sharing what degree of information. Later (even a few minutes later), upon further reflection, he can identify the steps in that process of knowing-*in*-action. Through reflection, he can consider the patterns of his thoughts in that situation and learn both about his responses and about his part in the dialogue.

Over time, participants in this kind of dialogue—especially if they are applying reflective practice alongside their dialogue work—become virtuosos in their adeptness and flexibility. As Schön puts it:

> What I want to propose is this: The practitioner has built up a *repertoire* of examples, images, understandings, and actions . . . *A practitioner's repertoire includes the whole of his experience insofar as it is accessible to him*

---

37. Schön, *The Reflective Practitioner*, 49. Emphasis original.

for understanding and action. When a practitioner makes sense of a situation he perceives to be unique, he *sees* it as something already present in his repertoire.[38]

What practices are in your repertoire? In the world of inter-religious dialogue, leadership, and education, situations perceived to be unique seem endless. Teaching cannot account for all possibilities; instead, inter-religious educators must instead help students cultivate the kinds of practices that will help them build their own repertoire of responses. We can consider dialogue practice—and reflection thereon—as models for ongoing incorporation into one's repertoire. In this way, not only does "reflection-in-action necessarily [involve] experiment,"[39] but:

> Each new experience of reflection-in-action enriches [the student's] repertoire . . . Reflection-in-action in a unique case may be generalized to other cases, not by giving rise to general principles, but by contributing to the practitioner's repertoire of exemplary themes from which, in the subsequent cases of his practice, he may compose new variations.[40]

The composition of new variations. What a holistic and encouraging metaphor for understanding inter-religious encounter. Experienced practitioners may offer "exemplary themes," but their larger task is to provide opportunities for practice, and equal opportunities to reflect upon that practice.

---

38. Ibid., 138. Emphasis original.
39. Ibid., 141.
40. Ibid., 140.

Practice, Posture, and Possibility
How to Practice a Posture of Openness

How might inter-religious educators facilitate these practices? Access to narrative pedagogies and participation in the kinds of activities Taggart, Wilson, McKernan, and Brookfield encourage will provide fruitful ground upon which students can build their practice. In particular, Taggart and Wilson identify three levels of how teachers engage with their work. They hold that reflective practice helps teachers engage at higher and more complex levels of practice and reflection. Taggart and Wilson articulate the following three levels:

> *Technical level:* reference past experiences; teacher competency towards meeting outcomes; focus on behavior/content/skill; simple, theoretical description;
>
> *Contextual level:* looks at alternative practices; choices based on knowledge and value commitments; content related to context/student needs; analysis, clarification; validation of principles;
>
> *Dialectical level:* addresses moral, ethical, or sociopolitical issues; disciplined inquiry; individual autonomy; self-understanding.[1]

---

1. Taggart and Wilson, *Promoting Reflective Thinking in Teachers*, 3.

One could apply these directly onto considerations of increased repertoire for inter-religious leaders. For example, novice inter-religious leaders depend to a greater degree on past experiences, including experiences from their own religious or ethical tradition. When considering how they feel about an encounter, they may focus on what happened in the encounter, without referencing power dynamics, notions of privilege, or a more complex self-understanding.

Some interview participants articulated possible stages of development when they described positive capacities in inter-religious education. That is, when describing categories of capacities, they often connected some skills with a sense of "beginning" in the process, and later or more developed skills with a sense of "getting better" in the process. For example, in continuing her reflection on "playfulness" as related to a kind of openness or humility that marks good inter-religious engagement, J. moves from talking about her own initial movements into inter-religious work as sparked by mere curiosity. J. reflects,

> So curiosity, playfulness. I think another layer that's not exactly an attribute that I always start my courses with is a focus on personal motivation for the work. There is such a range of motivations that bring people into this work. Speaking for myself, motivation can start out as fairly shallow. For example, I grew up in a family and community where Christianity was dominant and so there was kind of the fascination with other religions because they were so foreign to me.
>
> The positive of this is it sparked my curiosity and it led to a lot of other deepening commitments and concerns. This is increasingly something I want to understand in more depth, and apply to my own approach to interfaith work—the idea that curiosity is the essential first posture for interfaith work. It doesn't necessarily come naturally or easily to most of us.[2]

Using J.'s example, one possible "first posture" might be merely a neutral or slightly positive curiosity about something different;

2. J., in discussion with the author, October 2014.

perhaps, using R.'s examples, students would next be encouraged to *practice* engaging with difference and reflecting upon that developing practice. Indeed, the prevalence of site visits or immersion learning experiences as means for students to practice or cultivate a posture of openness speaks to inter-religious educators' understanding of how to help foster students' development from a beginning motivation for engagement into a fuller one.

C. serves as chaplain and instructor (in both the divinity school and in the religious studies classes) at a large, private university. Her students have a service learning requirement that takes them away from the more gentrified and less economically diverse campus neighborhoods and into the heart of their city. C. spent a few moments in the interview reflecting on how this requirement creates logistical challenges for the course instructors, but is worth it for the exposure and opportunities for reflection it brings the students. C. began by articulating why having the students engage with their wider community is necessary, stating, "This works best when people are doing it for more than just—you know, 'spectator sport' kind of interest."[3] A paraphrasing and clarifying question connected C.'s earlier comments about outcomes; C. was asked,

> So am I correct that in summarizing for the courses, one of the outcomes—is it exposure, exposure to these thinkers, to these leaders? Also exposure to things outside the ordinary rounds and also a connection between what they might be asked to do in the future and what you are offering?

C.'s elaboration demonstrates an articulation of development—from initial exposure, to recognition, to meaningful, demonstrated growth in leadership—that her program intends for its students. C. describes this progression, noting,

> Yes. And for the undergrads that exposure is important. But then also, just kind of challenging some of the assumptions. Or, for the undergrads' course, it's also as important to get them out into the community as it is to

---

3. C., in discussion with the author, October 2014.

introduce them to these concepts. Because if they come here and their only experiences are with the campus or some campus sponsored trip that they've done—these students are great at going around the world on [campus branded programs]. But to spend four years in a place and never go downtown, to never meet somebody who lives [here]—to think there's actually a reason to live in [this city] other than to be at [this university], and to encounter some of the realities that they have encountered in working with the community.

One of my students this semester is working with [. . .] a nonprofit that works to support families of murder victims in [this community], and releases prisoners. And so they organize prayer vigils. Whenever somebody is shot in gun violence in [the community], they organize the prayer vigil around for that person and that community. And this is important but you could completely live a sheltered [life at university] in [the] distance where you don't even know, or you are scared of going to [the city] because there's gun violence, rather than recognizing there are real people, and there are real conditions and there are systematic reasons—all of the things that go into play in those kinds of community relations.

I was joking with somebody last week, one of the biggest challenges I have in this service learning is getting them to their service site. Because they are so scared to take the bus anywhere. And where else do you meet the humanity in your neighborhood than on the bus? So I've had to, this semester if they don't have cars themselves then I had to figure out how to get them to their site because there's just this mental block around using the bus.

And there's a part of me that gets so frustrated by that then there's also part of me that gets it. You know most of the kids who at least come to this university have . . . never had to use public transport. And so why would they, probably, they want to use it here? And they want to think about it in terms of system economic discrepancies. They should think about, in terms of well—it's going to take us an hour to get to and from our service site if we have to take a bus. We could possibly dedicate an hour.

So I haven't quite figured out the teaching tool of how do they overcome that. Maybe I have to go with them and I have to say, "Okay, I'm going to do this with you the first time so that you can see how it is, you can see what it looks like." But this semester I'm taking an easier route just to help them find them cars. I've done this service to them by not [doing the work for them]. But that just speaks to the skills and talking about difference that they've learned through inter-religious work, or applicable [skills] across a broad range of difference.[4]

C. differentiates between the kind of traveling experience the university offers, where students stay in campus accommodations in a foreign city, with a more difficult local engagement that students find more challenging. She struggles with whether or not to make their exposure easier for them, wondering if part of the purpose of their required engagement is actually to participate in a new and different lived experience.

When she indicates that her choices to help them avoid public transportation do them a disservice, she points out that the skills they gain in (literally) traversing difference and moving from personal discomfort into a more nuanced understanding of their community are applicable, inter-religiously defined skills.

At the contextual level, we can imagine that an inter-religious leader with some repertoire of reflection and practice might have some knowledge and experience about practices, might be able to better articulate their own commitments, and have an increased vocabulary or set of models regarding analyzing the encounter. Similarly, more experienced inter-religious leaders can connect understandings of power and privilege, wider concepts of intercultural and sociopolitical issues, and a more nuanced self-understanding when encountering alterity. Throughout growth through these levels, consistent reflection may enable students to familiarize themselves with the tools they are using, even as they develop them.

4. Ibid.

Reflective practice is a rich set of methods and models for growing one's ability to think while acting, especially in situations that precede learning, which can be considered puzzles (Schön) or disequilibriums (Piaget). In professions where practitioners frequently encounter disruptions, difference, or alterity, reflective practice can provide both a means to become more adept at solving these puzzles, and better at their professions overall as their repertoires grow. In particular, educators and health care professionals have built upon Schön's work to address the specific needs and skills of their communities. Further research will uncover whether or not reflective practice is an essential skill for inter-religious learners and how, if it is essential, it can best be fostered.

Imagination and Seeing with New Eyes
The Power of Storytelling

In *Finding God in the Graffiti: Empowering Teenagers Through Stories*, practical theologian and religious and inter-religious educator Frank Rogers, Jr. links story creation, story sharing, and story hearing to the transmission of faith traditions, the development of one's sense of self, the mediation of experience of the sacred, the nurturing of a critical consciousness, the emboldening of the artist within each person, and the kindling of social transformation. In all of Rogers's conclusions we see the importance of cultivating story for reflective practice, and especially in his consideration of stories and critical consciousness development. In addition, because one purpose of this study is to examine how reflective practice might better foster inter-religious encounter, we shall also attend to the power of story as it relates to shepherding us through the shaky places of dissonance and difference.

In Rogers's title for the fourth chapter of his book, he asks, "How do stories nurture a critical consciousness?" He writes,

> In the same way that narrative is the primary form through which individuals make meaning of their experience, communities and cultures interpret events

through the lenses of their formative narratives. We may quest for true love, the American dream, the kin-dom of God, the blessing of Allah, global democracy, or multinational capitalistic domination, depending on the cultural narratives that shape us. Other people, communities, and cultures are interpreted as allies or enemies to the extent to which they promote or threaten such quests. How we engage those who threaten our pursuits, our "enemies" as it were, is also shaped by narrative. Stories form us toward either violent or nonviolent engagement with such people.[1]

The work of inter-religious educators explicitly involves facilitating encounters with and learning about "other people, communities, and cultures"; how we interpret alterity can mean the difference between violent, fear-based responses and relationships that support lasting educational and peaceful endeavors. Rogers notices in his teaching practice that narrative can claim and reclaim all of this. Perhaps, he considers, creating opportunities explicitly designed to build narrative capacity in learners will help them find their voices/vocations, share their perspectives in rich and enriching ways, and build community with justice and care. Rogers's work is resonant and flexible enough to be used by disparate and heterogeneous communities; although he personally identifies as a Christian, this personal context does not limit the recommendations of his work.

However, Christian religious educators often connect storytelling with the "capital 'S' Story" of the entrance of God into the human world through the life, death, and resurrection of Jesus Christ. The prevalence of the stories of Narnia, and their impact on generations of Christians, is one example—their author, C. S. Lewis, was a professor of literature, not a theologian, but his work with stories transcended popular culture and writing to make a lasting impression on Christian ministers and religious educators.

In *The God-Hungry Imagination*, Sarah Arthur tracks the history of writers of fiction and how story and imagination can be

---

1. Rogers, *Finding God in the Graffiti*, 99.

used to develop spirituality in young Christians.[2] Arthur differs from Rogers in that her recommendations for religious education are only suitable for other Christians—her practice in narrative pedagogy doesn't transfer easily into inter-religious spaces. When she wrote the book, Arthur was a young minister and divinity school student; her position as practitioner, working in a congregational context, allows us a glimpse of how sometimes it is authors, not formal theologians, who nurture the hearts in the pews. This is important for this study because we seek to understand which capacities are fostered and ought to be fostered by and in inter-religious education; this study posits that *reflective practice, deliberately nurtured by reflection via narrative*, is one possible way.

Christian religious educators have as a primary example the Story of the life and death of Jesus Christ. Dorothy Sayers, fiction writer, playwright, and essayist, discusses this double-edged possibility (story and Story) in her introduction to *The Man Born to Be King: A Play-Cycle on the Life of Our Lord and Saviour*[sic] *Jesus Christ*. Sayers notes the connection for her, as a Christian playwright telling *the* Christian story (yet in a drama), to the nature of the gospel story. Sayers writes,

> My object was *to tell that story* to the best of my ability, within the medium at my disposal—in short to make as good a work of art as I could. For a work of art that is not good and true *in art* is not good or true in any other respect, and is useless for any purpose whatsoever—even for edification—because it is a lie, and the devil is the father of all such. As drama, these plays stand or fall. The idea that religious plays are not to be judged by the proper standard of drama derives from a narrow and lop-sided theology which will not allow that all truth—including the artist's truth—is in Christ, but persists in excluding the Lord of Truth from His own dominions.[3]

Sayers exemplifies the connection many Christian religious educators see between practicing storytelling and story hearing with

---

2. See Arthur, *The God-Hungry Imagination*.
3. Sayers, *The Man Born to Be King*, 14. Emphasis original.

preparedness to practice reflection that can foster transformation. Arthur also includes the work of Lewis, J. R. R. Tolkien, Dorothy Sayers and Flannery O'Connor[4] as experts on how story pierces reality and touches readers and listeners in a spiritual place. These writers are connecting a posture of curiosity with a movement into transformation. For the purposes of this review of the literature, and for this study in inter-religious education, it is important to note that the aims of some Christian religious educators are not the same as the aims of inter-religious educators, although both may share the use of narrative pedagogy and reflection.

Notice that Arthur, in her work, identifies concerns of Christian ministers and educators even as she identifies how the metanarrative of the Christian story can answer that concern. Arthur writes, "I believe there's more going on, and the evidence is nothing less than the slow exodus of youth and their families from Sunday morning worship over the past few decades, no matter what new bells and whistles the church employs,"[5] and

> [We are experiencing the] loss of the communal story or "metanarrative" . . . Historically we've believed that our world's story is one that the God of scripture is telling, with a coherent beginning, middle, and end . . . we can no longer assume that post-moderns in the pews believe they inhabit a "narratable world."[6]

Arthur sees the power of storytelling as a balm to heal postmodern young people and bring them back into the church. Her book models the use of narrative pedagogy for her peers—similar ministers who decry losing youth and seek both to help them find

---

4. These fiction writers are sometimes known by Christian fans to be Christian, but, especially in the cases of Tolkien, Sayers, and O'Connor, their work is rarely overtly Christian or even religious. Arthur's point is that *storytelling and story consumption have the power to awaken reflective practice in us, which can lead to spiritual growth and transformation.* For our purposes, we are tracking how Christian religious educators use narrative pedagogy for religious education. Later, we will make the link from this to the possibilities of using reflective practice, via narrative pedagogy, for inter-religious education.

5. Arthur, *The God-Hungry Imagination*, 23.

6. Ibid., 25.

transformation and keep them in the pews. Unfortunately, their second point is neither necessary nor helpful for inter-religious educators or practitioners. In fact, if we follow Arthur's recommendations too closely, we end up with an exclusivity that truncates possibilities for dialogue and relationship with alterity. For example, Arthur shares an account of a young Japanese man who watched the movie adaptation of Tolkien's *Lord of the Rings* and then experienced personal (Christian) salvation at a Billy Graham revival. Arthur recognizes the transformative potential of Tolkien's work, but makes a move that no inter-religious educator would find palatable. She writes,

> Whoa. For youth workers who are generally in favor of telling kids the truth straight up, this sounds like a near miss. What if he'd gotten his hands on *His Dark Materials* by the decidedly anti-Christian Philip Pullman instead?[7] Or what if Billy Graham hadn't come to Tokyo? The guy could still be praying to El Whoever and wandering in a spiritual fog.[8]

Here we see the tension of Arthur's allegiance to one faith tradition—she is correct that stories have the power to draw Christian reflection in Christians, but hopes that the reflection and ensuing growth and development will remain [only] Christian. Similarly, Garrett Green writes, in his *Imagining God: Theology and the Religious Imagination*, "Imagination is the anthropological point of contact for divine revelation."[9] Might we also be able to say, "imagination is the anthropological point of contact for *human* revelation?" This book argues that exact point, and examines current inter-religious teaching and learning practices to discover whether or not this might be true.

---

7. In fact, Pullman's metaphor of "dust" from *His Dark Materials* can be used to help North American Christian students understand the material karmic concept of *pudgal* that makes up the more complicated aspects of Jain cosmology.

8. Arthur, *The God-Hungry Imagination*, 38.

9. Green, *Imagining God*, 43.

Imagination and Seeing with New Eyes

Frank Rogers and Susan Shaw both encourage reflective practices as a means to engage narratives more deeply. For example, in the field of religious education, both Frank Rogers and Susan Shaw both encourage reflective practices as a means to more deeply engage narrative. In *Finding God in the Graffiti*, Rogers connects the transformative potential of story-sharing and story-hearing with more contemplative practices; he writes, "narrative pedagogies can teach for *contemplative encounter*. Recognizing that some narrative texts have the power to mediate the presence of God, these pedagogies cultivate a profound indwelling of a story in the hope of experiencing the sacred reality embedded within it."[10] For religious educators, storytelling and story creation are rich mines from which reflective practice might emerge. Indeed, Schön's initial "trying to make sense of [the problem]" that leads one to access prior experiences is itself a narrative act. Shaw notes, "empirical research suggests that retrieval is actually a matter of reconstruction."[11] That is, we are not merely remembering something, we are reconstructing a story about that prior experience and telling it to ourselves. Just as reflection-in-action is a practice that can become a deeper and richer capacity over time, so are story-creating and story-sharing practices that lead to greater aptitude for reflection.

Narrative pedagogy closely informs reflective practice for two additional reasons. First, storytelling is a "process of self-creation and meaning making that is an important condition of learning."[12] The fact that it is a process is important—just as Schön's professionals encountered a disruption, cast back for related experiences, created a schema with which to address the puzzle, and artfully responded in the moment, the construction of a story includes casting back for experiences or prior knowledge, recognizing or constructing a schema for the new story, and sharing it responsively in the moment in a way that is accessible to the audience. Second, as Shaw points out, this process is a condition for learn-

---

10. Rogers, *Finding God in the Graffiti*, 18. Emphasis original.
11. Shaw, *Storytelling in Religious*, 24.
12. Ibid., 4.

ing, just as reflection-in-action (drawn from Dewey and Piaget) precedes learning. In addition, critical thinking is frequently held up by educators as an essential skill; reflection allows this capacity to develop, and allows it practice.

For example, in "Passing Over: A Model for the Use of Storytelling with Adults in Religious Education Based Upon the Hermeneutic Approach of John S. Dunne," Michael Edward Williams makes an observation about narrative thinking that hearkens directly to Schön's artfulness and McKernan's comparisons to artists. He writes, "Propositional thinking is logical, analytical, and abstract. Narrative thinking, in contrast, is imaginative, intuitive, and concrete."[13] While propositional thinking certainly has its place, spaces of great dissonance (for example, inter-religious encounters) call for *imagination, flexibility,* and *use of metaphor* to nimbly create new schema and allow participants to move past the puzzle and into learning.

In her book *Bridging Troubled Waters: Conflict Resolution from the Heart,* Michelle LeBaron describes both the power of metaphor and the varied ways educators and peacemakers can use metaphor as a tool, including enhancing communication and relationship, opening yet-unseen spaces of new possibilities in old conflicts, clarifying viewpoints, and connecting participants. LeBaron reminds us, "[Metaphors] help make explicit what are otherwise hidden: assumptions, perceptions, judgments, and worldviews."[14] Inter-religious education is not necessarily conflict-ridden for its participants, but many of us bring into educational settings limiting or limited frameworks that create "limiting assumptions, inhibitions, and emotional judgments."[15] As LeBaron puts it, "When we encounter mystery (and conflict is often mysterious, tangled as it is in relational, personal, and cultural dynamics), we seek to understand it."[16]

---

13. Williams, "Passing Over," 98.
14. LeBaron, *Bridging Troubled Waters,* 184.
15. Ibid., 188.
16. LeBaron. *Bridging Troubled Waters,* 188.

Indeed, in inter-religious encounters, *what one knows about the world comes into contrast with previously unknown*; alterity creates such dissonance that many participants either retreat into non-participation or avoid dialogue. And yet, these are ripe opportunities for growth. As Williams puts it, "Cognitive development occurs as ideas or assumptions come into conflict, making simplistic answers no longer viable."[17] Cognitive development requires that our assumptions come into conflict. *To develop as humans, we must encounter differences that disturb us.* Many of us have experienced this as our worlds widen to include relationships and encounters with those dissimilar from us. One task of inter-religious education is to facilitate encounters and relationships in ways that allow participants to move past a craving for simplistic answers and to sit in a place of provisional, flexible, or imagined possibilities. Williams reminds us, "Learners who are able to see commonality in disparate characters and situations may come to accept differences as not only tolerable but also positive."[18] Is this not one aim of inter-religious programming and education—to help participants accept differences as positive and affirming?

Inter-religious encounter ought to be a place in which participants can practice the best, most imaginative and most fruitful versions of human development. Storytelling can be a palatable practice that can scaffold places of reflection, creation of new schema, and the creation of new answers to old puzzles. Inter-religious engagement can foster a multiplicity of stories—leading to rich reflective practice and an increased posture of openness. As Williams notes, "The more stories, the more standpoints. The more standpoints, the truer to the complexities of human experience."[19] The wealth of resources teachers have for practicing ongoing reflection-in-action speaks to their understanding of the value of "more stories, more standpoints." The natural next step would be to apply this notion into fostering

---

17. Williams, "Passing Over," 62.
18. Ibid.
19. Ibid., 103.

this understanding for students—indeed, their stories and standpoints are ready to be shared.

For example, in an inter-religious setting, one task for participants might include the following: think of a time when you wondered about what happens after death. Instead of beginning with a dialogue between adherents of different religious and ethical traditions *about* the afterlife, participants are given a chance to consider their viewpoint from the place of story, their own stories. *This posture of storytelling can keep curiosity and wonder in the space longer, and can forestall judgment and too-early conclusions.*

Cultivating one's "learners' eyes" means to practice a flexible posture of learning, to cede—for short periods of time—one's position as expert in hopes of coming at a dilemma from an unexpected perspective. One might think that all students—whether pre-service teachers, nursing students, or students in an interfaith studies course—are naturally using learners' eyes, we must also remember that this is a practice, and all of us find ourselves more or less adept at it, and more or less aware of our status as learners, depending on how safe we feel, the degree of relationship we have with our classmates, whether or not our beliefs are threatened, and what our aims are for participating in the class. *While it feels good to be an expert at something, it can induce vulnerability to maintain learners' eyes.* One role of educators and facilitators may be to create "safe-enough"[20] containers for practicing this vulnerability. N., a Christian professor with teaching roles at both a seminary and in a business school, describes how his students demonstrate places of vulnerability, even as he names how this is one of the key purposes of inter-religious education:

> And it seems to me, that's the amount of risk in an engagement like this . . . is that it becomes an "undone"

---

20. Lev Vygotsky's "zone of proximal development" articulates a specific, ineffable place between total comfort and paralyzing fear—teachers should facilitate students' movement into this space, where just the right amount of dissonance positively provokes learning and some degree of mastery is still possible. A totally safe space would not foster enough disruption for transformative learning to take place, but neither is extreme provocation helpful for the development of new ways of being.

sort of experience. How is this going to change you as a student in your curriculum and then in your ministry, on the one hand, or your work with an agency, as a leader [on] the other?[21]

N. is trying to capture what happens to students when they encounter dissonance; they come "undone" (perhaps, the experience as "undone" is less easy to manage?). He also affirms that being changed is one obvious and essential aspect of successful inter-religious learning. This embrace of risk or uncertainty also appeared in N.'s descriptions of why we teach inter-religiousness. He notes:

> Fostering trust between people, beyond the kind of voluntary networks that people choose for themselves, and building new networks. That's the challenge of inter-religious engagements . . . So, helping people be reflective about those limits, about the ways our discourses and practices narrow options for us, and then recognizing commonalities—across the things we call our traditions and recognizing the differences . . . But these things are fluid, they are malleable, they're strategies that migrate and discovering how they migrate and where they migrate, and then intentionally engaging our traditions in behalf of the deepest purpose, which is to eliminate violence, is the real challenge before us.[22]

Similarly, J. connects a positive side of vulnerability, one that can open learning spaces to joy or playfulness; she describes the positive attribute of vulnerability, or openness in her response to my question about what helps students succeed in her classes and programs. J. shares,

> When I see them stepping out and taking leadership, that's when I feel like, what we are trying to do educationally is working. Because I think it requires an openness and a quality of playfulness. These are qualities that allow folks to engage with enthusiasm in learning about

21. N., in discussion with the author, October 2014.
22. Ibid.

something that's new to them, something that's unfamiliar. Something that someone else might react to with a sense of fear or a sense of its "otherness."[23]

J.'s assertion that playfulness stemming from an openness—as opposed to fear—is related to R.'s desire that his students fall in love with difference. One way teachers and facilitators can evoke experiences that foster places of positive vulnerability is to model perspective-taking practice.

Finally, the lens of colleagues' perceptions encourages us to practice perspective taking. For many, the ram's horn is essential for marking the new year; it has always been a symbol of the high holy days. How is it seen by that person's colleague, who eschews all animal products because she believes every living being's soul is equal? If one can successfully enter into an experience from a new point of view, not only do we learn something new about the experience, we learn something new about our colleague and about ourselves. When he returns to his reflection on the symbol of the ram's horn, it now includes the more nuanced inclusion of his colleague's perspective. In this way, reflective practice becomes a multi-faceted model for engagement and relationship.

We adults avoid vulnerability. We cling to the notion that we have it all figured out. We have a worldview, it's based on our knowledge and experience, and it is deeply uncomfortable for it to feel threatened. Indeed, we do feel threatened when we encounter information that runs counter to what we think we know. Examples might include:

- Marriage is between a man and a woman, and lasts a lifetime
- Abstinence and then monogamy are the only ways sexuality should be expressed
- Women and men are fundamentally different, and should do different things
- There is one God, and Jesus is the one Way, Truth, and Light
- There is one God, and Allah is His messenger

23. J., in discussion with the author, October 2014.

- "His" is the appropriate pronoun for God
- Children need two parents
- "American" means white
- All women want to have children

Then, over time, we meet other people. We taste new foods. We have crises, and our colleagues and neighbors help us. We travel. Bit by bit, we get exposed to new ideas. Often these can begin to manifest in thoughts like:

- He's one of the good ones
- He's gay, but he's not immoral
- They actually are quite nice, even though they're foreign
- She doesn't go to church, but she's a decent woman
- She's divorced, but she's very moral
- They're atheist, but they seem like wonderful parents
- My colleagues are Mexican, but they're very hard-working
- I met him at Habitat for Humanity: he's Jewish, but we get along great
- I believe homosexuality is wrong, but she's my sister and I love her and her partner

Of course, unfortunately, many of us avoid information or experiences that cause us to experience dissonance. We avoid new foods, we avoid travel, we never attend a religious or ethical service different from ours, we read websites that tell the news from our perspective, and we follow on social media those most like us.

How do we start where we are and move into changing the world? We need to:

- Move beyond "Religion 101" classes
- Actively facilitate discomfort
- Use relationships and similarities as foundations for radical change-making

- Borrow helpful frameworks from other fields: Dismantling racism, working for economic justice, gender and dis/abilities awareness.
- Keep asking: Why should we try to understand people who are different?

I have always been naturally curious. Curiosity about anything can grow into positive interfaith engagement. For many people, their knowledge about the wider world comes from books, even fiction. If you're a book lover, think about the worlds you loved the most: were they English manors or gardens, such as *The Secret Garden*? Were they countrified family settings, including *Little House on the Prairie* or *Anne of Green Gables*? Did you catch glimpses of Europe or the Caribbean, or first consider Native Americans in stories of the West? Our abilities to picture other children, other people, and other families wholly—including what they eat and wear, how they fight, grieve, mourn, and fall in love, how they treat the very young and the very poor, how girls and women and those with disabilities are treated—all of this imaginative work can prepare us to be more open to religious and cultural differences.

For many of us, fictional worlds are the first places we begin to practice other points of view. Folk tales, fairy tales, cultural myths, and children's books are filled with varieties of living creatures: animals who can talk, interact, and create; aliens both benign and frightening; dragons, living dinosaurs, and monsters; and (most importantly) girls and boys like us, but in very different situations. We experience different time periods, different kind of houses and homes, different types of parents, and different roles for children.

When I was young, three particular stories resonated with me, and I frequently imagined myself as their protagonists. I believe these three stories helped shape who I became as an adult, as a mother, scholar, theologian, and teacher. I read and re-read *Pollyanna*, *The Secret Garden*, and *The Little House on the Prairie* countless times. In my own backyard, I playacted being on a moor, discovering hidden gardens, and encountering kindly strangers who could change my life. When I couldn't sleep, I piled on layers of clothing and made pretend hot potatoes to put at the feet of my bed, pretending I had to survive a blizzard and wondering how I could stay warm enough to sleep through the night. I didn't know anything about the English class system or expectations for children, but I felt earnestly for Collin and Mary, and recognized my own curiosity, fears, and longings.

Reading and talking about stories can be a natural place to investigate—even for the first time, even purely for pleasure—other points of view. In fact, storytelling and storysharing can be a container and space for *reflective practice*, which we know is a key ingredient for interfaith learning. *Why do we relax when we listen to a story? How can this pleasurable practice translate to developing our capacities in perspective-taking practice and tolerance?*

Let's think about the process of engaging in a story. First, we choose the book, the setting, and the way we engage. Are we listening to a book on tape while we run? Nestled next to a grandparent on the front porch? In a hot bath with a thick library book? Re-reading a childhood favorite in a busy bookstore? Even reading the back of a novel we'd never usually choose in an airport gift shop? The simple fact that we have agency and choice in both content and setting feels good to us—this comfort can offset any feelings of confusion, frustration, or annoyance once we begin reading. Even a dense, difficult text, or one that we've been assigned to read, can be less frightening than an encounter with a stranger if we choose where and how to read it. For stories in particular, because they are meant to be pleasurable, we have even more of this natural prevention against painful disequilibrium.

Second, if we are readers, beginning a new book or settling back to hear a story is a practice in which we have engaged other times. Like walking a labyrinth, beginning a *puja* or recitation of the Rosary, or any other contemplative or spiritual practice: we know how this works. We know how it feels to sit, open the book, begin reading, relax, engage with the characters, learn more about them, plan ahead to find more time to read, dog-ear or mark passages that are appealing, wonder about the narrative, share ideas from the story with others, feel the latter half of the book get "smaller" and realize we're finishing, either feel glad that we're finally finishing or wistful that the story is coming to an end, finish with satisfaction, sadness, or delight, and recommend the book to others. "You *have* to read this" is a kind of evangelism that is still welcome and celebrated in all circles today. Finding kindred spirits through stories that you both enjoy is relational.

When new books in the Harry Potter series were coming out, I was living in New York City and commuting every day. There was something wonderful about seeing, on every train platform and in every subway and bus, hundreds of strangers all with the new copy that had just become available. People from all walks of life: men in business suits heading to Wall Street, teenagers riding the train uptown to the Bronx, women with small children in strollers, older people with a coveted library copy. New Yorkers don't talk to one another while commuting. Very occasionally, one stranger might ask another: "Where are you? Chapter . . . ?" and share a deepened moment of connect. "Ahh! Yes, could you believe when . . . ?" and then both would hush, both because it isn't done to talk to strangers, and also to avoid spoiling it for the dozens of other strangers on a train car. The great religious stories used to be shared currency in this way, and plays and touring minstrel music before that. The narratives which we crave, consume, and seek to share are powerful containers for us to lay our trust and in which to grow our capacity to wonder.

Finally, in fiction we meet others who are not like us, and we imagine—in a confined space, time, and format—their points of view. Through fiction, we experience miscarriages and death, famine and miscarriages of justice, migration and betrayal. In stories, we imagine marching as foot soldiers, failing as aging courtesans, losing our ability to communicate. Good stories help us experience being human in ways our bounded, everyday lives necessarily limit. We may feel curiosity, disgust, anger, or even terror when we encounter alterity in fiction . . . but we are "safe" to remain with the story.

In contrast, many feel intimidated by beginning conversation with a stranger, let alone someone from a different place in the world, or with markedly different ways of understanding the world (reflected in clothing, choice of body adornment, language, or other nonverbal markers). The fear parts of our brain seek out difference and attempt to paralyze us. But in storytelling, we are suspended in a kind of hammock of safe curiosity. We remain in the other's point of view for as long as we're in the story-hearing state. And like in any practice, the more we do this, and the longer we spend in this state, the better we are able to suspend our judgment and find new and different points of view in which to engage.

What would happen in your community, if instead of building a "Religions 101" series, you promoted a book club to grow perspective-taking practice? Fiction for Dissonance, say. Discomfort through Art. What if your outcomes were not explicitly related to, say, welcoming Muslim immigrants or building a sanctuary congregation, but were focused instead on foundational skills and postures that must precede that work (and that many of us still lack)? Possible learning outcomes for this kind of book club might include the following:

- Practice reading for pleasure, and practice identifying and articulating why and when reading is pleasurable
- Self-knowledge about the kinds of characters we like, appreciate, connect to, fear, or wish to emulate
- Connections with personal life, community life, political life, and the text
- Ability to articulate differences and contrasting opinions
- Practice picturing the world from various characters' points of view—and the ability to picture the world from their point of view for sustained periods of time
- Increased comfort reading the world through others' eyes
- Increased curiosity

- Ability to transfer the skill of having a posture of openness to other areas (consuming news media, trying new restaurants or markets in different parts of town, suspending judgment long enough to keep from defriending someone or deleting a tweet)

Sometimes, "interfaith engagement" can be daunting. You might think you need to know something about religion, or about group facilitation, or about other cultures. You might also feel like you're not "Christian enough," or "Buddhist enough," or "Pagan enough," to represent your own tradition at an interfaith event.

But most of us can handle sitting in a comfortable environment, enjoying coffee and snacks, and talking about a book (or short story, or long-form magazine article, or movie, or even album). Think about conversations you've had about summer blockbusters or a parenting article that gets shared on email and social media—you have an opinion, you feel comfortable disagreeing (the stakes feel lower), you make natural connections to other ideas, actors, or similar stories or concepts. You feel animated, sharing your likes and dislikes. It's enjoyable to share your opinion, and hear what others think about an experience in common.

If others in your community are interested in building your capacities for perspective-taking practice, consider holding a book club. Pick something fun to read or watch, and work to find really character-driven pieces. Practice asking, "What was going on in that scene/chapter/encounter?" and "What did you see that makes you say that?" and "What else is going on?" Have fun. Look forward to these events. Share food and drink. Remind yourself that all of these practices, all of these questions and encounters—they are the work of interfaith engagement, and all of these skills are transferable.

These skills include:

- Perspective taking practice
- Imaginative capacities
- Openness to another's experience

- Compassion and empathy
- Articulation of point of view
- Dialogue

These are practices.

Looking at and experiencing art can similarly help you hone your perspective-taking abilities. Art is a mirror upon which you gain practice and virtuosity in the following skills:

- Reflecting
- Articulating
- Listening
- Being open to difference
- Understanding

All people are much more interested in what each other has to say, than in what the teacher, facilitator, or religious leader can *tell* them. Art is open-ended, and can always be returned to—we can always look again and find more. Three questions in particular foster perspective taking, and building the practice/capacity for holding multiple points of view in one's mind:

- What's going on in this picture?
- What do you see that makes you say that? (evidence)
- What more can we find? (no "one right answer"—open to multiple, ever-unfolding ideas)

These questions, and art as entry point, also facilitate shared, community meaning-making. Something powerful happens when we look together, share our ideas, and foster/practice dialogue as we look/think/share together, in real time.[24]

Using art to facilitate dialogue is richer, and less conflict-driven, because it's not two people *facing* each other, having to say what they think, and confronting difficult ideas. Instead, it's us looking

---

24. These questions are the foundation of a curriculum and facilitation process called Visual Thinking Strategies, or VTS.

together, and putting disparate ideas into the room, and hearing them even as we have our own idea. The brain's capacity to look, hear difference, and look again is like a muscle that grows, and art continues to provide a helpful surface upon which this growth can be reflected back, leading to rich meaning making.

Personal story is essential to the way we relate to the world. Resilience is tied into to our sense of self, a through-line of personal narrative that tells us where we are in the world, and where we're going. People who live in violence and conflict, in places of fear and violence, their narrative through-lines become fragmented. This also happens to communities and families. Neighborhoods, for example, can experience fragmented identities, and the richness of shared history and experience is lost. Some of the most powerful work we as teachers, artists, and activists can do is create *spaces* and model—help folks articulate their "small stories," listen and receive them. And art is such a powerful prompt, impetus for starting this process.

"What do you see that makes you say that?" is not only a question about what in the art the person sees, but what the *person* sees, and what's going on in his/her interior space to lead to that observation. And, our small stories fit into a "grand narrative," a shared story about a neighborhood, or a city, or the human condition. And feeling that strand—how my own self fits into the whole—is hopeful. It gives us a sense of agency and purpose.

So, in a sense, this work prompts much more than merely *looking*. It is an example and then a modeling of self-reflection and then engagement, via perspective taking, *entering another's imaginative space*, and then dialogue and relationship-building. As learners involved in interfaith engagement spend more time, relationship, and practice with these skills and dispositions, they will develop the leadership and facilitation skills to help other groups or members of their communities engage these practices.

As facilitator, you have the opportunity to shepherd discussion, help learners access and review material, and build lasting interfaith learning and engagement in your community. Be mindful of the particular needs and gifts of your community, and adapt accordingly. Collaboration and learning are rarely linear endeavors, so feel empowered to incorporate recommendations when and where they fit your needs.

How to facilitate dialogue events (including book clubs, art walks, story sharing events, shared spirituality events) and ways to prepare:

Review the materials. Highlight things that will be of interest to your group, especially things that may be in the news, might be unfamiliar, or might create debate or spirited discussion in your group. If there are names, terms, or locations less familiar to you, take some time to look those up—and then consider sharing the resources you use with the group. Model having a posture of openness and making inquiry a practice.

Check in on the discussion forums that your group is active in—are there unanswered questions or concerns? Any misinformation or opportunities for deeper learning that can be corrected or fostered? Consider adding questions to the discussion forums that relate to the life of your community—to the week's sermon or message, to local news or concerns, to the lives of those within the group.

Take some time for yourself to reflect—maybe you do this through physical activity, through gardening or cooking, or through reading fiction or creating something new. The brain needs recess to successfully incorporate new ideas; this is especially true for leaders and facilitators. Your time doing something (seemingly) unrelated will benefit your experience in the group by allowing your brain time and space to process and link to new ideas. Remember, reflective practice is an essential ingredient in inter-religious learning.

Recommended activities for time together:

Self-reflection, storytelling, and connecting the course materials to key texts and aspects of your tradition are good ways to both continue the learning participants are doing in the courses on their own, and build upon new concepts and practices. Consider the following possible activities:

Gallery walks: Provide a written prompt (including one from a journal entry or discussion forum post within the course), each participant posts an answer on a long table or along a wall. Then, in silence or to quiet music (no talking), participants "walk" along and read the answers of others. They can use additional pieces of paper (Post-it notes) or write directly on the texts, to respond, ask questions, affirm, or make connections.

Think/pair/share: Start by letting participants take a few minutes to journal, sketch, or write silently. Then, let participants work in pairs to share their ideas. Finally, one member of the pair can share some key ideas to the entire group. One benefit of this is that no one person has to share her own story, and pairs can combine viewpoints or ideas, or leave out identifying information.

Spotlight: Have learners bring in a quote, image, headline, or even one part of the course from the previous week to share for further query and discussion. Sometimes, having something concrete to examine together can help answer questions and enrich learning. These "artifacts" can be collected and displayed over time to create a kind of collage to document ongoing inquiry and learning.

Connect to context: Invite deliberate connections from the course material to part of your shared context: meaningful teachings from your tradition, developments in your geographic location, something related to the age, gender, or professional interests of your group. For example, in a course on understanding power and privilege, you might seek out an article or resource on how differences in culture play out in leadership and management; this type of scaffolding allows participants to connect their new learning to their contexts and bring their own personal expertise and experience into the learning space.

Possible hot topics / "ouch" moments:

Many adults struggle with two things that can come up in these kinds of encounters: feeling pain or guilt about having participated in conflict or oppression, and encountering ideas that are contrary to their current worldview. For example, if I have been taught all of my life that people who believe in God are conservative, uneducated, and want to work against women's rights, and I encounter materials that show this might not be the case, I might feel anger, confusion, a need to be "right," and grief at the loss of some of my older ideas. *These feelings of "being disrupted" are all essential parts of learning.*

Setting guidelines for how to listen and talk—using "I" statements; using phrases like, "ouch" when something unexpectedly emotional comes up, to communicate to the group; being willing and able to take breaks—can be useful tools to prepare in advance for these moments.

If a participant brings up a question or topic that feels "hot," you might consider asking the group, "Has anyone else had that question or thought? What was your experience with it?" For example, someone might wonder aloud if all Muslims are violent. If you take the opportunity to ask if others have wondered about that, you might invite other participants to share why they once thought that, if and when they encountered information to the contrary, and how their thinking changed or became more nuanced. Sometimes, letting people talk first in pairs, or letting people write or sketch ideas, before sharing with the whole group can help defang ideas as well as provide essential context for fruitful sharing and dialogue.

Finally, remember that you don't have to have it all figured out in one session, or during one educational program. It is okay to leave a session without having all of the answers, or even feeling in agreement, or even feeling like successful dialogue took place. We humans learn over time, and dialogue is relational—it takes time for the essential ingredients of relationship to take place and foster transformative dialogue. You might not see the fruits of this learning all at once.

What if the session seems to be falling apart?

What to do when we don't have all the answers: Three key things to remember when trying to address questions that seem hard to answer.

- Learning together is *always* better than one person giving all of the information. We will never know everything about all traditions—and there are an infinite number of text resources to find specific answers. The more important, transferable skill is to learn how to learn, together. Practice naming aloud what we are wondering about, practice identifying resources, and practice finding ways to look, and look again—these are all skills that we can apply to other contexts.

- "The person with the most power speaks last." This fundamental teaching in inter-religious and inter-cultural learning reminds us that issues of power and privilege intersect in every context. If we are mindful about who has more and less power, and work to open and maintain spaces for voices to be heard, then we can often surface new and different ideas with which to work.

- Take care in making minority voices the experts or teachers for everyone in their tradition. No group is monolithic. In addition, people who are in the minority within one group can get "fatigue" from always having to be the teacher or the source of information. Consider Googling or asking friends or leaders within your own community first—some things are easily found.

Also consider how you set up the room—giving people surfaces on which to write can facilitate one sort of learning, while sitting on couches and comfortable chairs can foster another kind of conversation. As a peer facilitator or co-learner, try to avoid using a lectern or microphone—this will set you apart as an "expert" and discourage full participation by some.

If leaders in your community participate, try and make sure they are not set apart—for example, holding the session in your head minister's office, where she sits at her desk and the rest of the participants sit in chairs around her table, can signal differences that aren't helpful for this kind of learning.

If you are interacting with others from different religious or cultural communities, be mindful of different ways men and women interact, different ways some people show respect (physically, with eye contact, to those of various ages), and that different people have different needs and requirements regarding sharing personal information, talking about difficult subjects, or wanting to be able to leave the setting and return.

If you're doing a multi-part series, you might consider using time in the first session to talk about the following: learning styles, expectations, fears, hopes, concerns, and ground rules for how to ask questions, how to make sure everyone participates (in ways that feel right and appropriate), and what commitments the group expects. Talking about these differences in learning styles and expectations will be related to the ideas and practices that emerge in the learning outcomes.

Some ideas for fostering this learning within your context include:

- A special table during coffee hour for extra time to chat or a place to share questions, carpooling, or technical information
- Flyers in the community newsletter or bulletin boards that share updates on the group and even additional resources that come out of the group that might benefit the wider community
- Readings that support difficult conversations and transformative learning
- Asking hard questions "within" first (for example, if a Christian and Jewish community is taking the course together, two Christian participants might ask clarifying questions of one another before going to their Jewish colleagues—this can help communities share how members get accurate information and prevent "fatigue" or unintentionally giving offense.) Many groups find social action or community engagement a natural outgrowth of this work. Ideas for continuing this work might include:
- Partnering with another religious or cultural organization for community building or social justice work
- Organizing around an issue in your community, like hunger, homelessness, racism, or ecological justice

- Connecting with wider interfaith movements, either on the local or national level
- Continuing study, either through a text study or by inviting speakers
- Working with local media to feature positive stories of interfaith collaboration and peace-making

Suggestions for topics, themes, and ways of fostering engagement also include:

- Good questions for ice-breakers and discussion include: What does "diversity" look like in our community? In your own life, how have you gotten along (or not) with one another? Do you think religions cause conflict? Why are you interested in interfaith engagement? Do you think learning about other traditions might make you "less" of your own tradition? What key texts, teachings, or examples from leaders that you value encourage engagement with others?
- Ask participants to share how they or their family arrived in this community, state, or country. As participants share, track on a map or sheet of paper all of the original points of departure and entry. Then, if people feel comfortable sharing, ask them if they have always been part of their current religious or ethical tradition. What diversity do you already have in your group?
- "Holy envy" can refer to a wistful feeling about another tradition's practice—you might feel "holy envy" for the way some Christians are able to speak directly to God in a way that doesn't happen in your own tradition, or have "holy envy" for elements of fire, incense, flowers, and tangible parts of worship in Hinduism that your practice lacks. Notice together where moments of "holy envy" arise, and think together about what is appealing, and whether there are unexplored aspects of your own tradition or practice that could be renewed or re-evaluated.

- Consider visiting a restaurant, museum, performance event, or worship service (if applicable) of a culture, religion, or tradition different from yours. Food, art, and music can often be "entry points" to practice being open to difference.

- Imagine someone from outside your context is visiting for the first time. What would you want them to know? What are the key practices they should try? Is there anything they should not do, as an outsider? If you were designing a welcome service to your group or community, what elements would you feature?

Note: It can be painful for many of us to come to terms with elements of our privilege. Two key points are important to remember in this process. First, those in the minority are not responsible for either affirming or forgiving us, or for teaching us about their culture or viewpoint. Second, all pain is valid and we don't have to compare our experiences with privilege and marginalization. Part of learning to listen without evaluating can mean listening without needing to compare. Consider checking in with the group if emotions surface, and remember that aspects of difference and dissonance are valuable, natural, and precede deep learning.

Issues of power and privilege underlie and intersect interfaith work. If we want to build interfaith relationships, and foster understanding, we must directly address issues of privilege. These include gender, race, ethnicity, culture, language, dis/ability, sexuality, and economic status. Questions each of us must ask, and that can be fruitful for religious and interreligious settings include:

- Who leads in your context? Is leadership representative of all of the voices of those who participate?

- Talk about "social location" for participants in the group. Are most of you from similar backgrounds and circumstances? Do any of you live, work, worship, or have family in differing circumstances? How do you navigate differences in social location in various places in your lives?

- What do your important religious or ethical traditions or teachings have to say about power, about the marginalized, and about inclusion?

- How can those with more power in your community work to facilitate greater inclusion of other voices?

- Take a walk around and through your setting (workplace, worship space, campus, dining or study area) and try to see the space from various perspectives: What are the primary languages and means of communication in use? How can those with differing physical abilities navigate and thrive in the space? Do you have to own something to access the space (membership card, library card, religiously-based fees, knowing someone in the community)? Are all parts of the space accessible to everyone (are children, or those who aren't ordained, allowed in all spaces?) Are parts of the space divided for use by certain genders? Are images (portraits, stained glass, photographs) of only one type of person?

- Talk about times when members of your group have felt particularly welcome in new setting, and when they have felt like they didn't belong. (Some examples might include visiting a new country, a new type of restaurant or gym, an expensive boutique, trying to get legal or civic paperwork, first day in a new school or workplace.)

- Make a list of top five movies, television programs, popular novels, or pieces of popular culture. Work to identify whether those featured in those works are more or less diverse. What bodies and physical attributes are represented and celebrated? What skills or intellectual attributes? Genders, ages, ethnicities, or religious perspectives? In the coming weeks, look for examples of inclusive examples of popular media, and bring them back to the group.

Interfaith work is more than dialogue—it is the art of listening, and sharing. When bridge-building must lead to relationship, storytelling can provide places and spaces for real and lasting engagement. Community leaders and organizers have long understood the power of amplifying the voices of their constituents, and attending to the voices of those often unheard. This course provides participants with examples of the power of storytelling, practice identifying and working with key themes of good storytelling practice, and space to reflect upon their own stories—and how they can bring about positive change.

Questions for reflection and discussion around storytelling include:

- Why do the phrases "Once upon a time" and "Tell me a story" evoke such a consistently positive response from so many, across age and social groups?
- In your religious or philosophical tradition, what is one of the primary stories that gets told and retold?
- As a child, what was your favorite story?
- Think of a time when you recently went unheard. (In a relationship, on social media, at work, in a political or healthcare setting, as an employee or learner, etc.) To whom where you speaking? What got in the way of that person or group receiving your story?
- Do you feel comfortable speaking your mind, even in uncomfortable situations? What skills does it take to share a perspective even when it's not easy?
- Open the discussion for participants to ask clarifying questions about any material covered in the course or to explore in conversation journal entry prompts or activities that were especially interesting (or confusing!) for the participants.
- Consider finding a way to highlight and capture oral histories in your community. Many elders go long days without being heard, and many of us could benefit from learning from their experiences. At the same time, children and youth also want to be heard. Consider planning a series of listening events. Who could you invite? What theme might foster rich story-sharing? Are there religious or spiritual texts that could

provide context for such an event (e.g., "Hear, O Israel . . . ")? What are helpful ground rules that would foster maximum participation and inclusion? How can you document the event and share it with the wider community?

Finally, many interfaith leaders and practitioners have found the following resources to be helpful in their own work:

Judith Berling: *Understanding Other Religious Worlds: A Guide for Interreligious Education*

Mary C. Boys and Sara S. Lee: *Christians and Jews in Dialogue: Learning in the Presence of the Other*

Francis X. Clooney *Comparative Theology: Deep Learning across Religious Borders*

Catherine Cornille: *The Im-Possibility of Interreligious Dialogue*

Paul F. Knitter: *Without Buddha I Could Not Be a Christian*

Michelle LeBaron: *Bridging Troubled Waters: Conflict Resolution from the Heart*

Jennifer Howe Peace, Or N. Rose, and Gregory Mobley, editors: *My Neighbor's Faith: Stories of Interreligious Encounter, Growth, and Transformation*

Frank Rogers, Jr.: *Finding God in the Graffiti: Empowering Teenagers through Stories*

Susan M. Shaw: *Storytelling in Religious Education*

Chris Stedman: *Faitheist: How an Atheist Found Common Ground with the Religious*

In Conclusion
Will Uncertainty Save Us?

Being human is hard. We are made to be in relationship with each other, and yet we are capable of causing such great harm and pain. Language can excite and inspire us, and yet also has the capacity to diminish, legislate, and oppress. Do we really understand one another? Is it possible to give up comfort and certainty in hope of greater community and flourishing?

Being human is all we have in this life (to use my own Christian language). We can choose to avoid puzzles, resist messes, and continue to consume media and pursue relationships that affirm only the world as we see it.

We have the potential to encounter new information and incorporate new knowledge and experience into our meaning-making. We have the potential to be transformed by difference. And we are very often enriched by our relationships with others, even when—nay, *especially when* they are different than we are. If you only take one key learning away from this book, let it be this: disequilibrium precedes *all* learning. If you haven't felt uncomfortable, you haven't truly learned. And if you resist discomfort and uncertainty, you are denying yourself the chance to be transformed. "Educate" means to "lead out." As a teacher or religious leader, you have the responsibility to help lead communities out from places of fear and resistance, and into relationship and wholeness. And as fully human participants in this human race, you have the opportunity to seek ways to lead yourself out of being paralyzed by difference, and experiencing true, transformative learning. Stop resisting uncertainty. See it, name it, nod in recognition—it's an invitation to learning and to growth.

Bibliography

Arthur, Sarah. *The God-Hungry Imagination: The Art of Storytelling for Postmodern Youth Ministry*. Nashville, TN: The Upper Room, 2007.
Berling, Judith. *Understanding Other Religious Worlds: A Guide for Interreligious Education*. Maryknoll, NY: Orbis, 2004.
Block, Jack, and Adam M. Kreman, "IQ and Ego-Resiliency: Conceptual and Empirical Connections and Separateness." *Journal of Personality and Social Psychology* 70, no. 2 (1996) 349.
Boekaerts, Monique. "Coping in Context: Goal Frustration and Goal Ambivalence in Relation to Academic and Interpersonal Goals." In *Learning to Cope: Developing as a Person in Complex Societies*, edited by Erica Frydenberg, 187. Oxford: Oxford University Press, 1999.
Boys, Mary C., and Sara S. Lee. *Christians and Jews in Dialogue: Learning in the Presence of the Other*. Woodstock, VT: Skylight Paths, 2006.
Brooks, David. "Putting Grit in Its Place." *The New York Times*. http://www.nytimes.com/2016/05/10/opinion/putting-grit-in-its-place.html?mabReward=A4&action=click&pgtype=Homepage&region=CColumn&module=Recommendation&src=rechp&WT.nav=RecEngine&_r=0.
Clooney, Francis X. *Comparative Theology: Deep Learning Across Religious Borders*. Malden, MA: Wiley-Blackwell, 2010.
Condly, Steven J. "Resilience in Children: A Review of Literature with Implications for Education." *Urban Education* 41 (2006) 211–36.
Cornille, Catherine. *The Im-Possibility of Interreligious Dialogue*. New York: Crossroad, 2008.
Dewey, John. *Logic: The Theory of Inquiry*. New York: Henry Holt and Co., 1938.
———. *Principles of Instrumental Logic: John Dewey's Lectures in Ethics and Political Ethics, 1895–1896*. Edited by Donald F. Koch. Carbondale, IL: Southern Illinois University Press, 2008.

Bibliography

Garmezy, Norman. "Vulnerability Research and the Issue of Primary Prevention." Paper presented at the Annual Meeting of the American Orthopsychiatric Association, San Francisco, 1970.

Green, Garrett. *Imagining God: Theology and the Religious Imagination*. Grand Rapids, MI: William B. Eerdmans, 1998.

Masten, Ann S., and Auke Tellegen. "Resilience in Developmental Psychopathology: Contributions of the Project Competence Longitudinal Study." *Development and Psychopathology* 24 (2012) 345–61.

Masten, Ann S., and J. Douglas Coatsworth. "The Development of Competence in Favorable and Unfavorable Environments: Lessons From Research on Successful Children." *American Psychologist* 53, no. 2 (1998) 206.

Maugham, W. Somerset. *The Razor's Edge*. New York: Vintage International, 2003.

McKernan, James. *Curriculum Action Research: A Handbook of Methods and Resources for the Reflective Practitioner*. New York: Routledge, 1996.

Mudge, Lewis S. *The Gift of Responsibility: The Promise of Dialogue Among Christians, Jews, and Muslims*. London: Bloomsbury Academic, 2008.

Pargament, Kenneth I., and Jeremy Cummings. "Anchored by Faith: Religion as a Resilience Factor." In *Handbook of Adult Resilience*, edited by John W. Reich, Alex J. Zautra, and John Stuart Hall, 193. New York: The Guilford, 2010.

Peace, Jennifer Howe, Or N. Rose, and Gregory Mobley, editors. *My Neighbor's Faith: Stories of Interreligious Encounter, Growth, and Transformation*. Maryknoll, NY: Orbis, 2013.

Puett, Tiffany. "On Transforming Our World: Critical Pedagogy for Interfaith Education," *Cross Currents*, http://www.crosscurrents.org/Puett2005.htm.

Rogers, Frank, Jr. *Finding God in the Graffiti: Empowering Teenagers through Stories*. Cleveland, OH: Pilgrim, 2011.

Sayers, Dorothy L. *The Man Born to Be King: A Play-Cycle on the Life of Our Lord and Saviour Jesus Christ*. San Francisco: Ignatius Press, 1990.

Schön, Donald A. *The Reflective Practitioner: How Professionals Think in Action*. New York: Basic, 1984.

Schoon, Ingrid, ed. *Risk and Resilience: Adaptations in Changing Times*. Cambridge: Cambridge University Press, 2006.

Shaw, Susan. *Storytelling in Religious Education*. Birmingham, AL: Religious Education, 1999.

Stedman, Chris. *Faitheist: How An Atheist Found Common Ground with the Religious*. Boston, MA: Beacon, 2012.

Taggart, Germaine L., and Alfred P. Wilson. *Promoting Reflective Thinking in Teachers: 50 Action Strategies*. Thousand Oaks, CA: Corwin, 2005.

Tough, Paul. "How Kids Learn Resilience," *The Atlantic*, http://www.theatlantic.com/magazine/archive/2016/06/how-kids-really-succeed/480744/

Waters, Everett, and L. Alan Sroufe. "Social Competence as a Developmental Construct." *Developmental Review* no. 3 (1983) 80.

Bibliography

Williams, Michael Edward. "Passing Over: A Model for the Use of Storytelling with Adults in Religious Education Based upon the Hermeneutic Approach of John S. Dunne." PhD diss., Northwestern University, 1983.

www.ingramcontent.com/pod-product-compliance
Lightning Source LLC
Chambersburg PA
CBHW070924160426
43193CB00011B/1572